CHOLA ✕ PANDYA

THRONE WARS

MARKETING LESSONS FROM THE ART OF WAR

PRAVIN SHEKAR

INDIA · SINGAPORE · MALAYSIA

Notion Press

No.8, 3rd Cross Street
CIT Colony, Mylapore
Chennai, Tamil Nadu – 600004

First Published by Notion Press 2021
Copyright © Pravin Shekar 2021
All Rights Reserved.

ISBN 978-1-63781-632-5

This book has been published with all efforts taken to make the material error-free after the consent of the author. However, the author and the publisher do not assume and hereby disclaim any liability to any party for any loss, damage, or disruption caused by errors or omissions, whether such errors or omissions result from negligence, accident, or any other cause.

While every effort has been made to avoid any mistake or omission, this publication is being sold on the condition and understanding that neither the author nor the publishers or printers would be liable in any manner to any person by reason of any mistake or omission in this publication or for any action taken or omitted to be taken or advice rendered or accepted on the basis of this work. For any defect in printing or binding the publishers will be liable only to replace the defective copy by another copy of this work then available.

Can fiction help you learn? **Can a marketing book be so interesting that you can't put it down?** If this sounds preposterous, then this book will prove you wrong.

Venkatarangan Thirumalai
Technology Entrepreneur & White-space leader

* * *

A thought-provoking book that transects across millennia, while drawing inspiration from each era. Reading it reminded me of the Panchatantra - a gripping storyline that keeps you engaged, while extracting a take-away from each. **As an entrepreneur & a bit of an Indology buff, I found the analogies from the Moovendhar especially valuable!**

Gopinath Gandhi
CEO, ReferralYogi

* * *

This book contains fantastic analogies on war strategies that can be used in business. I particularly liked the part how the character Agastyan, the Coach of Rajaraja Cholan prods him in the right direction thus enabling him to find his solutions. **The power packed marketing lessons from history are all relevant to current day marketing needs.**

Sangeeta Shankaran Sumesh,
Business Coach & Bestselling Author

* * *

How did the Tamizh kings of yore strategize, learn and adapt when they fought wars and annexed kingdoms or won back lost territory? Pravin weaves together the intriguing tales of the War of Cholas and Pandyas. He takes us through victories, setbacks and comebacks, carefully gleaning out powerful marketing strategies from these stories in his own simple, lucid style. **The kind of book you finish at one go but ponder over for days on end!**

Jayashree V
Educationist

* * *

This book with its richly developed contents from cultural and historic examples, not to mention biz comparisons, influences thinking instead of preaching. The stories are spine-tinglingly realistic that **it's almost as if Pravin travelled to such a time and place, escaped from it, and then just wrote it all down**.

Sujitha Arvind
Architect, Author

* * *

An eclectic selection of war and wisdom. Pravin has once again outdone himself and brought out the battle strategy of yore and applied it to modern boardroom war fare. Vibrant penning of stories, interwoven with the trials of the moovendars and JK playing the modern day Chanakya. **A book meant to enthral the historian, the businessperson and the common reader alike.**

Revathi Sanjeev
Creative Entrepreneur

* * *

Contents

Introduction 11

Sun Tzu, Cholas and Pandyas............................ 13

The Narrative Flow... 15

Prelude 19

MOOVENDHAR: The Trio 19

SECTION 1
REVENGE IS SWEET.
OR IS IT?

Chapter 1   Playing with Perception......................... 23

               MOOVENDHAR: Setting the Base 30

Chapter 2   Fools Rush In. What About You? 33

               MOOVENDHAR: The Written Plan 39

Contents

Chapter 3	Alliance as the Way Forward	46
	MOOVENDHAR: A Question of Alliances	53
Chapter 4	What Will You Do Once Your Strategy is Known to the Enemy?	58
	MOOVENDHAR: Pricing, Defense and Attack	65
Chapter 5	When Big Attacks Small: What to Do?	69
	MOOVENDHAR: Business Wars and Preparation	74
Chapter 6	A Cornered Tiger is Most Dangerous	77
	MOOVENDHAR: An "Almost Victory"	83
Chapter 7	Strategy is Grammar, O Marketer	83
	MOOVENDHAR: Fight the Right Fight, Well!	95

SECTION 2
REVERSE REVENGE

Chapter 8	The Lull after the Storm	101
	MOOVENDHAR: A Relay Race for Muscle Memory	106
Chapter 9	Winds of Change... Spark a Wildfire	109
	MOOVENDHAR: Strategy	114
Chapter 10	Short-Term Alliances for Long-Term Growth?	117
	MOOVENDHAR: Outlier Alliances	122
Chapter 11	Stay on the Cutting Edge, Literally	125
	MOOVENDHAR: What You See is False!	131
Chapter 12	The Final Chapter	134
	MOOVENDHAR: Helicopter Leadership, Anyone?	141

Contents

SECTION 3
A PEEK INTO THE FUTURE:
PANDYAS VS SOUTH INDIA!

Fight the Fight within, First 147

The (Marketing) Warrior without Vanity 154

About the Author – Pravin Shekar 157

Thanks 159

Other Books by Pravin Shekar 161

Introduction

This is a fictionalised presentation influenced by the lives of the Chola and Pandya kings, who ruled vast parts of Southern India many centuries ago. Those days, rulers were forever trying to expand their kingdom, and were always on the quest for new lands to annex. This led to many a war. The history of India is replete with colourful stories involving ambitious rulers, wily court strategists, brave commanders and guerilla warfare, all of which make for compelling reading even today.

Not just that. They carry many important, timeless marketing lessons for business leaders.

This book is a collection of a few such stories with a few such lessons, which will be useful to corporate leaders, entrepreneurs and marketers. It is for them that I have written this book.

Tamizhakam (the Tamizh-speaking regions of India) saw the rule of four main dynasties: Cheras, Cholas, Pandyas and Pallavas. They flourished during the last

Introduction

few centuries of the BCE (Before Common Era) and the first millennium of the CE (Common Era). Among them, they ruled much of what we know as South India today, and were famous for their might, statecraft and military strategies. I have taken a small sliver from the history of two of those dynasties, Cholas and Pandyas, and of the Hoysalas, a powerful dynasty that ruled many parts of present-day Karnataka.

While I have taken the characters from the history of South India (of which I am a tiny part), I have drawn inspiration for some of the strategies and learnings from Sun Tzu's ancient classic, "The Art of War". The interpretation and learnings mentioned in each chapter are those that I strive to implement for my business and those of my clients. I believe they will help you in your business, too.

I have taken the storytelling route because stories land better in our hearts and minds, and stay there for a long time. The stories, incidents and dates mentioned here may not exactly correspond with factual accounts of history; I have taken a few creative liberties with them. Please remember this if you think you have spotted any errors herein — in names, places or dates.

Sun Tzu, Cholas and Pandyas

Sun Tzu. He was a military strategist, general and writer who lived in ancient China (5th century BCE). His writings and lessons are valid even to this day. They have been translated into many languages and interpreted in various contexts. His treatise, "The Art of War", is the basis of several marketing strategies and business books.

The Cholas. Reputed to be one of the longest-ruling dynasties in the world, they lorded over a large part of present-day South India. At the height of the dynasty, the kingdom extended even to present-day Indonesia, Malaysia and Sri Lanka. Their headquarters was in Tanjavur and places around it. They, along with the Cheras and Pandyas, formed the moovendar ("trinity of rulers" in Tamil) of South India.

The Pandyas. Headquartered in Madurai, they were contemporaries of the Cholas. Their quest for supremacy in South India saw them fight many tough wars with the Cholas, Cheras and Pallavas. All these dynasties were known for their just rule and their patronage of literature, art and architecture.

The Narrative Flow

Each chapter in this book is laid out in three parts. The first part describes war stories and strategies from South Indian history. The second part contains my interpretation of these in the contemporary business context — as applicable to start-ups and established companies in any domain. The next part of each chapter is a section I have named "Moovendar". This Tamil word is a combination of the words "moondru" (three) and "vendar" (kings).

Historically, "Moovendar" refers to the triumvirate of Chera, Chola and Pandya (kings). But the Moovendar referred to here are CEOs of companies, who talk about their current situation, their challenges and the decisions/approaches they need to take. Each chapter ends with a marketing example that corresponds to the chief learning from that chapter.

The purpose of this book is to give you a direction for the interpretation of each story. After that, it is up to you, dear reader, to implement the learnings in your business/career.

* * *

> **Glossary of terms for business interpretation**
>
> War = Battle for a market
>
> Enemy = Competitor
>
> Region/Kingdom = Market/Territory
>
> Ally = Partner

Seething with rage, he wanted to destroy everything within reach.

The young man was distraught.

He walked up to the mountaintop to digest the news.

His King, his leader, his guru – dead!

The note said that his King had been killed – butchered – and his army, decimated.

His King, who had had grand plans and had sent him as an emissary.

Looking into the distance, he was thinking how, why, what next?

What next, was clear to him.

> **"I will avenge the death of my King!"**

Prelude

MOOVENDHAR: The Trio

The three CEOs meet in a café. A startup, Beachville Café in Chennai is a hub for coffee meetings. Our moovendar were school mates who remain friends even today. They meet regularly to discuss their respective businesses, analyse situations and hash out solutions.

Anu runs a startup that provides healthy sandwiches on a subscription model. It is a two-year-old firm with a set of regular clients, and is now gearing up to expand significantly. Anu has ten people on her staff, and faces the usual pressures of a startup: lack of time, money and other resources.

Gokul runs Klingo, a services company that wants to scale fast. He wants to move to the next stage. He has 150 people in his firm, spread over three offices. His main challenge is that he must change the direction of his ship (read company) even as it keeps moving!

Prelude

Rita runs Ricata. Ricata is a software products company that has clients all over the globe. It is on a scaling-up run, and is forever hiring and expanding. 400 people work for the firm across the world.

JK is Anu's, Gokul's and Rita's business mentor who answers their questions and guides them in the right direction, helping them find their answers.

SECTION 1

REVENGE IS SWEET. OR IS IT?

Chapter 1

Playing with Perception

"Victory will be mine today. The enemy is fleeing. Bloody cowards, making me chase them to death. They are fools, attempting an attack on my fortified location. A fort that my family has held for ages. I will teach Sundara Pandyan a lesson he will never forget."

The Pandyas and Cholas had been legendary rivals for centuries. Land and power swapped hands often, like a river in spate claiming the fields along its banks. Whenever a border — especially an unmarked one — is shared by two kingdoms, it leads to heightened tension. It is like a festering wound, giving no peace to either kingdom! And this happened frequently with the Pandyas and Cholas.

The 13th century seemed to belong to the Pandyas. Their ascendancy was marked by the capture of several regions, including smaller kingdoms. Their vassals began to grow, as did their prosperity.

With prosperity come two things that directly contradict each other — contentment and greed.

Sundara Pandyan I, the ruler responsible for the resurgence of the Pandya dynasty, was pleased and pissed. Pleased at the growth of his empire. Pissed at the one thorn that remained lodged in his flesh — the Chola chieftain, Kulothungan (Sundara refused to call him a king, since he thought that the power of the Cholas had been severely curtailed).

"That Kulothungan refuses to give up his last bastion in Uraiyur. I need to get the better of him to ensure my supremacy over this region and the longevity of the Pandyas."

Kulothungan belonged to that set of people who refused to face reality. In their mind, they were the lords of all that they surveyed. Refusing to see the truth, they built their castles in the air and lived in the cocoon of their past glory. What he lacked in strategy and manpower, Kulothungan made up for in pop and spite. He sent letter after letter, calling the Pandyas cowards, lepers and impotent — swear words of yore.

Sundara Pandyan called his commanders, Manickam and Velan. His instruction was simple. "Bring me Kulothungan's head. It is time to weed him out of my kingdom, and I entrust this responsibility to you. Before the next full moon, I want this done."

Manickam and Velan smiled at each other. This was the opportunity they were waiting for. Battle-hardy veterans, they knew which fights to pick and which ones to walk away from. They sometimes walked away from battles if it did not make sense to fight them. Which is why their enemies called the Pandyas cowards. This was the buzz being spread among the populace: the Pandyas will run away from a fight. Where's the valour in that? How can "brave" sons of our soil walk away from a challenge or war? Cowardice is the only explanation and all Pandyas, therefore, are cowards and losers.

The stereotype stuck, but Manickam and Velan knew they had the confidence of their king, Sundara Pandyan. Sundara knew the power of strategic attack, defense and retreat.

The taunts from Kulothungan continued to come thick and fast. Manickam sent back a message saying Sundara will attack the Cholas within a week. He added that the attack would be big, and that no quarter would be given. Fair warning, but it made Kulothungan laugh. The enemy was coming to him, to *his* bastion, to *his* region, where he reigned supreme. AHAAAAA! Victory will be mine, he thought.

Sundara's two commanders reached Kulothungan's region and camped near the horizon. Just out of sight, even when seen with monoculars. News reached Kulothungan that the enemy had arrived with 100,000 soldiers. Even those claiming loyalty to Kulothungan had apparently switched allegiance.

The first night of the siege, shivers ran through Kulothungan's people. They saw the entire Southern side of their region lit up. Sundara Pandyan had indeed come with 100,000 soldiers! So many people and so many fire torches! All that the Cholas could do was wait.

Two days later, Kulothungan's minister came running to him.

> "Sire, did you notice? The number of torches is less today."

Kulothungan rushed to the tower of his fort to see. It was true; the number of torches was visibly less. What was happening? Could they be planning a rear attack? He ordered additional sentries to the North.

Two days later, they noticed that the number of torches had reduced further. It appeared that Sundara's forces were about 40,000 now.

By the sixth day of the siege, Kulothungan's spies came back with the information that only 10,000 of the enemy forces remained. It looked like the rest of the troops had deserted Sundara Pandyan. The alliances he had forged seem to have cracked on the battlefield.

"These Pandyas were always cowards. Just look at them. They cannot keep an army together. Hahahaha!"

The seventh night, they could ascertain that the Pandyan forces had dwindled to much less than

Kulothungan's. And the next morning, his spies said that the enemy had decamped! They were turning back.

Kulothungan readied his army, all set to attack the fleeing enemy.

> "Victory will be mine today. The enemy is fleeing. Bloody cowards, making me chase them to death. They are fools, attempting an attack on my fortified location. A fort that my family has held for ages. I will teach Sundara Pandyan a lesson he will never forget."

It was midday when he gave his commanders the green signal to leave the fort. The chase was on in earnest. There was a pep in his soldiers' step. Kulothungan led the attack himself. They had to traverse a ravine, and it was dusk by the time they reached this narrow passage. Steep cliffs all round, and the faint light dancing all around them. They reached a turning point. A tree marked the location where they had to turn to get out of this area. One of the soldiers pointed to the tree, which had a flag tied to it.

Curiosity always provokes a response. Kulothungan reached the tree, lit a torch and saw something etched on the tree. Peering closely, he read:

> **"Kulothunga Cholan, under this tree, today, you will die!"**

He recoiled, shocked. Before he could say anything, his body was punctured by arrows, and he died that day, under that very tree. His army was attacked by archers perched on top of the ravine.

How did this happen?

Manickam and Velan had formed a think tank to arrive at a strategy to vanquish Kulothungan. They decided to play on the stereotype that the Pandyas were cowards.

"If they think of us as cowards, let us make use of that perception!" said Velan.

Often, deception is key to victory.

They went in with a force of only 5,000 warriors. Messages and a disinformation campaign, though, created the impression that they had a 100,000-strong army. To reinforce this impression, Velan's men lit 100,000 torches and scattered them across the horizon. This gave the Cholas the impression of a vast army waiting to attack them. As the days went by, the number of torches and tents were reduced. It led the enemy to think that cowardice had set in — the soldiers were deserting the Pandya camp.

When Kulothungan gave chase, everything had been planned. The day and time of the attack, and the place through which the enemy's army would be led. Velan knew that they would have to go through a ravine, and that it would be dark by the time they reached the tree.

Curiosity killed the cat. And several men, including a Chola ruler!

Kulothungan lay on the ground, his body punctured by arrows. His life flashed in front of his eyes.

Oh, I wish, if only I had...

This story was inspired by Sun Tzu, and the story of the war between the Wei and Chi kingdoms. I have adapted it to South Indian history.

* * *

INTERPRETATION

The leader needs to know his men well, train them well. When the leader is genuinely courageous, he will have the courage to show false weakness. He and his men will have the discipline to feign confusion in the ranks. It is all about playing up a perception and using deception to win with a small force.

The true general knows that the goal is to win with minimal loss of his own men and limited bloodshed in the enemy camp.

MOOVENDHAR: Setting the Base

Rita: I have this big competitor, and I am entering his territory in Germany. But if he gets wind of my entry, he will snuff me out. He has a stranglehold on his clients.

Anu: Don't we all have this problem? We need growth, but cannot let the competition know our ambitions or plans. How long can we remain in stealth mode?

Gokul: I have a couple of anchor clients, but I have to be wary of competitors' attacks on them. What do I do?

JK: Rita, how many clients do you need to make a dent? You need to seek them out and draw them in, one by one, until you hit the necessary critical mass to go public. Plan a big campaign and spread the word that you are expanding in France. Increase the number of offices — your fire torches! Just like Sundara Pandyan did in this story. Divert the attention of your big competitor till you gain the time you need to secure a few key forts (clients) in Germany.

Anu, I know the stakes are different for you. But the logic remains the same. What's the point in going big bang in your communication? Leave ego and vanity metrics aside. It will be best if you had the cash flow to sustain your bootstrapped growth. For that, you need revenue. You need to build your micro-market and get a set of steady, recurring, paying customers. You need a set of carefully curated clients, who will invest continuously in your journey. Yes, you will take up some non-strategic clients and tasks, but only if the money is good enough. It is ok to be in hiding till you can emerge with a big army of money and people — in truth or to create the perception of strength.

Gokul, you are entrenched well; which means there will be continuous attacks on you. You will feel it when you get a little complacent in your relationship with your clients. Do not let vanity lead your decision-making. Like the Cholas, do not get enticed into smaller battles that the new competitors will want to draw you into. Build a substantial moat around your clients and deliver so much value that you remain top-of-mind, always!

Marketing case in point

2003.

Albert Heijn (AH), a Dutch grocery chain was losing customers to its competitors, Aldi and Lidl.

It decided not to get into a direct battle, but kept running its business as usual, with a focus on the mid-price market. Competition was priced 3-6% lower than AH.

After a lot of secret planning (even its own store managers did not know anything about it), AH struck. It announced significant price cuts and communicated this widely through advertisements.

Competition didn't do much for some time. But after seeing a spurt in AH's growth, they too dropped prices. AH continued to surprise competition by cutting price in specific categories, one category per week. Competition was forced to cut back their profits and offer deep discounts. AH let them bleed. In the summer of 2004, it dropped prices by up to 35% on more than 1500 products! It had everything planned, having negotiated price concessions from all of its suppliers.

Competition was beaten, and by 2005, AH was back to being No. 1.

Chapter 2

Fools Rush In. What About You?

REVENGE.

Sundara killed my father. I will avenge my father's death.

Revenge in the heat of the moment is that much sweeter.

Rajaraja Cholan III was the son of Kulothungan III. His father was killed by the Pandya king Sundara Pandyan I while he (Rajaraja Cholan) was away.

By the time Rajarajan returned to their capital, everything had been lost. His people, his father and his kingdom. All gone!

His mother and family had escaped through a secret tunnel. Rajarajan met them at a pre-decided location. His mother was livid too, and wanted revenge. She goaded Rajarajan. "It was our valour, our lineage, our right — you need to seize all that back."

Rajarajan was charged up.

So he did what any 20 year old would do. Rush in. He cobbled together a small band of soldiers left over from the pillage in the ravine.

"That coward Sundara and his commanders attacked my men from the top. We were trapped in a ravine, and their archers fired away. Is that a way to win a war? Where's the sportsmanship, the fairness in that?" thought the incensed youngster.

His small platoon attacked Sundara's forts and towns. They attacked everything in their way; such was the murderous rage, the hunger for revenge. Anger-lust. A time and place where there is no scope for reason; only for wild action. Rajarajan found out where Sundara Pandyan was. He marched with his army through the forests and got ready for a surprise attack on the Pandyan king and his troops.

"We will strike them like lighting, take revenge and take over the kingdom!" So went Rajarajan's pre-battle talk to galvanise his small force. A mix of soldiers young and old, a few blacksmiths and other assorted youngsters, craving for action. They planned to attack at dusk, when the Pandyan city would be winding down — a time when sentries would be tired. When one shift would be ending, and tired soldiers would be handing over the baton to another group for the night.

The path in front of them had trees that hid their approach. The Cholas moved forward stealthily.

Sundara's guards were relaxed; some even seemed drunk.

"Hahahaha! Drink on, my enemies. I am your death approaching." Rajarajan could sense his impending victory.

His troops inched closer to the enemy forces. This was turning out to be so easy! They were about to strike when the "sluggish" Pandyan soldiers jumped up with alacrity.

Rajarajan and his forces heard a sound from behind.

Turning around, they found that they were being attacked from the rear by Sundara's forces! Their surprise element was gone — in fact, it had never been there.

Sundara's spies had spotted Rajarajan's army much earlier. They then allowed Rajarajan to enter their land and smell victory. The rage of revenge, combined with the perception that the Pandyan soliders were drunk and their security lax, made the Chola king drop all planning and rush in for the kill.

It was a whipping Rajarajan would never forget. Sundara did not even send his chief commanders, the valiant Manickam and Velan. It was Mugilan, a junior captain, who lead their army. The organised manner of their attack ensured that Rajarajan's ragtag troops panicked from the get-go. Their formation broke, soldiers rank helter-skelter. They stopped following orders and went about purely on instinct, doing what they felt like doing. Chaos. Is this what the vaunted Chola army had come to?

The Pandya soldiers were smiling as they attacked the Cholas. They had won the war in their head even before setting foot on the battlefield. They knew Rajarajan was trapped: boxed in from all sides.

Mugilan spotted Rajarajan, and they entered a one-to-one combat. Both of them were of the same age, more or less, and exchanged blow for blow. It was a matter of time, though. Rajarajan had traveled from afar, and had been in battles and skirmishes all the way through. On the other hand, Mugilan was fresh and better prepared for this fight.

A vigorous swish from Mugilan sent Rajarajan's sword flying. The Chola scion found himself stepping back without any defense. Mugilan picked up a spear and, with a big shout, hurled it at Rajarajan. Rajarajan was a prince of the Chola dynasty. He would not cower in the face of defeat or death. He knew both were coming his way in the form of the spiraling tip of Mugilan's spear. He squared his shoulders and faced the spear.

In the nick of time, Rajarajan's friend and commander, Vikraman, dove between the spear and his prince. He gave his life to save Rajarajan. In the ensuing confusion, Rajarajan slunk away.

He escaped and ran back, tail tucked between his legs. Tears streaming from his eyes, he sneaked into the jungle. The Pandyan soldiers entered the forest and started a manhunt. Sundara Pandyan wanted Rajrajan dead. Rajarajan hid in the hollow of a tree and did not step out for an entire day. More than the fear of death, it was defeat, disgrace and humiliation that made him hide.

He roamed around the jungle aimlessly for a few days. He questioned himself about the recent events, and the actions taken by his father and himself.

"How could I rush in without any preparation? What was I thinking? Now, more of my men are dead. And I will be labelled a coward for leaving the battlefield!"

My father rushed into the chase and was trapped in the ravine. I didn't do any better!

Why did I not set up my own spies, front and back?

How could I attack without a strategic plan? Without an escape route and backup plan.

What can I do now? My objective is still clear: avenge my father's death, and resurrect the Chola name and empire.

* * *

INTERPRETATION

When an unprepared leader goes into battle — without a plan or enough knowledge about competition — defeat is certain.

Do you have your marketing plan in place? If you need a basic framework, please visit www.pravinshekar.com/ThroneWars and download a template.

MOOVENDHAR: The Written Plan

JK: So, do you have a written business plan?

Anu: No.

Gokul: Sort of.

Rita: Yes...but it hasn't been updated in a year.

JK: So all of you are flying by the seat of your pants. Blaming the economy and others when things go wrong. And taking credit for success (when things go well), without knowing or analysing why and how.

"Oh, I didn't know that" has killed so many initiatives! So write down your business plan now. Here, use this template to make a bare-bones business plan.

Purpose: What's the purpose of my business?

Me: Who is with me?

Us: Who can I partner with in my network? Who are my allies?

Them: Who is my competition? What is the ecosystem I am playing in?

How: How can I set up an attack and defense strategy?

When: What's the timeline?

How much: How much time, money, resources am I planning to invest?

Measure: How will I measure if my business plan is working or not?

* * *

Anu:

What's the purpose of my business? What's my objective for the next year? (Purpose)

I am a startup, and I need to establish a subscription business with a consistent, predictable revenue stream. I am a boot-strapped entrepreneur, and I need to reinvest my profits for growth.

Who do I have with me? (Me)

A small team of ten. Each member is a Jack of all trades, handling production, customer support and a bit of marketing.

What partnerships and alliances do I have? (Us)

I have my raw material suppliers and my distribution partners. We have two social media influencers, who like our product and write about it. Machinery, packaging, logistics are all in the works.

What environment am I a part of? Who am I competing with? (Them)

Given the perishable nature of our product, we operate only in Chennai. We are growing, though, as the demand is increasing. With better packaging and logistics, we can deliver in other cities, too.

We need to make more people aware of our products. We also have a few B2B deals with hotels and other institutions.

How do you intend to set up an attack and defence strategy? (How?)

Right now, we need more people to know about our product. So we need to communicate our value proposition, the fact that it is an entirely vegetarian product line. We need to get through to the people who need to first know about us and then try our products.

As regards our defense, we are still building our market share. What's there to defend?

What are your timeline and objective? (When?)

In one year, we need to have at least 250 subscriptions.

How much time, money and other resources do you have to deploy? (How much?)

I am investing my own money. So every rupee needs to stretch to the limit.

How will you measure ROI? (Measure)

By the number of subscriptions.

* * *

Gokul:

Purpose: I need to reorient my company to a growth mindset. I am in the services business, and there is an ebb and flow. I need greater predictability.

Me: A team that has been with me for a long time. Each member knows their role but also steps in for others, when needed. I've partnered with an HR firm to bring in talent, as and when we need it. We also have a couple of international tie-ups to provide our services to them and their clients. One of them represents us in Europe.

Them: I am in a commoditised market now. It is all about the lowest price. With many more players entering the market and the economy being what it is, there is constant pressure to deliver inspite of dropping prices and margins. My clients understand, but they have pressure from their procurement and pricing teams.

How? I need a good defense strategy, as every bid is a street fight. We invest a lot in travelling, meeting clients, pitching. And yet, we lose out. This happens even for projects that we executed regularly earlier but where we are now facing pressure.

I need to expand my clientele in order to grow. We are investing in social media marketing and SEO. That's our attack plan.

When? One year to set the ship right (to a growth orientation), and get my forecast and cash flow in order.

How much? I am looking at growing the marketing team and increasing the number of client touch-points.

Measure: The number of deals won and longevity/retention of the deals.

* * *

Rita:

Purpose: Scale. I want to be the No. 1 in my industry. I need to grow by 200%. Now.

Me: I have a strong, growing team of more than 400 members spread over several locations in the world.

Us: We have many partnerships: software tools, sales, resources, partnerships with like-minded companies, consultants.

Them: The SaaS market is cut-throat. The environment is ultra-competitive. Our clients are constantly on the look-out for the next big thing. My competitors keep a close watch on what I do.

How? We are always under attack, and need to defend our market share and our client relationships. When competition lowers prices, we need to do so, as well.

We are fighting for the same set of clients, and our attack and defense strategy is to build superb relations with our clients.

When? One year. 200% growth. And then some more. I have a Board to report to, and a bunch of investors.

How much? I am funded. Whenever I forecast a need for growth, I raise funds. There is a team working on this. I have it all at my disposal. I just need growth and scale.

Measure: Growth. That's it.

JK: Ok. Good start!

Marketing case in point

A $65 million faux pas!

A huge market that has recently opened up to the world. This is what the decision makers at Kellogg's headquarters thought about India in the early '90s.

Keen to harness the potential of what they saw as a large market, they entered India with their range of breakfast cereals. They were confident that the "healthy" cereals would quickly supplant the oily parathas, pooris and vadas from the Indian breakfast tables. As it turned out, Kellogg's wasn't able to make a dent in the market. Their cereals simply did not take off, even after years of high-octane marketing that positioned their products as healthier breakfast options.

They failed because Kellogg's did not understand the Indian consumers and their eating habits correctly. The brand wanted to introduce a new eating habit, replacing the hundreds of hot and spicy breakfast options that Indians are used to with bland cereal that was to be had with cold milk. And the products were expensive!

With sales sinking, Kellogg's went back to back to the drawing board to study the market and its habits anew – and try again to see how to ease into the Indian psyche. And the Indian belly.

Chapter 3

Alliance as the Way Forward

"Oh, there you are! The Coward Prince."

The words stung Rajarajan's ears. The voice sounded familiar.

In the days after the battle with Sundara Pandyan I, Rajarajan walked through the forest endlessly, seemingly in circles. Battered, bruised and almost broken, he hardly resembled the strapping, angry young man he had been before the battle started. He was lost in thought, re-analysing his loss to Sundara Pandyan's minions.

Being solitary for a long time made him think about his purpose in life. A solo walk in the woods does make one wonder what, why and other such existential questions.

He knew he had to seize what was rightfully his. He needed to rebuild his forces. And for that, he needed assistance. He decided to seek it.

Alliance as the Way Forward

One day, he was rudely awakened from his beauty sleep under a mango tree. Two burly men held his arms. Another big, moustachioed man stood some distance away, hands akimbo and a stern look on his face. He was scrutinising Rajarajan.

"Who are you? What are you doing in this kingdom?" asked Kirathagan, the moustachioed man.

"I am Rajarajan, heir to the Chola kingdom."

Rajarajan was shocked at what happened next! The three men started laughing their guts out.

"Yeah, you are the Chola King, and I am Yama's messenger!" said Kirathagan.

(Yama: the God of Death in Hindu mythology)

No amount of convincing worked. Rajarajan was tied up and marched to a fort adjoining the forest. He was dragged through the main hall and presented before the king.

"Who are you, and why do you claim to be someone you aren't?" asked the king.

The voice was familiar. Rajarajan raised his head and his eyes slowly focused on the person asking the question. He was silent for some time before croaking:

"Sire, it is me. Rajarajan. We met a few months ago."

The king got down from his throne and walked up to the young man. He brought his wizened face close to the youngster and turned his head towards the light to see him better. A few moments of silence, and then recognition dawned! Yes, this young man had come to his palace some time ago.

The old king was Narasimhan III of the Hoysala dynasty. The Hoysala kingdom was situated north of the region ruled by the Pandyas. Narasimhan placed his hands on Rajarajan's shoulders and smiled.

"Indeed, it is you, young prince. What a change in the last few months! What happened was unfortunate. Tell me more about it."

For the next couple of hours, Rajarajan narrated all that had transpired since his last visit to Narasimhan's palace. He added that fate had decreed that they had to meet again under these sad circumstances. He said that just before the men had captured him, he had anyway been planning to meet Narasimhan to seek his help.

"Help for what, young man?" asked Narasimhan.

"To avenge my father's death and seize my kingdom back."

Narasimhan was silent for a while. The old king knew that these reasons were superficial. War was not something to rush into. He asked Rajarajan to rest for a few days and recoup his strength. Rajarajan was accommodated in the royal quarters. Shaved, bathed and well-rested, he was walking around the fort the following morning when he heard the voice.

"Oh, there you are! The Coward Prince."

The words stung Rajarajan's ears. The voice sounded familiar.

He looked around, but saw nobody. The voice teased him again.

"Look at him run with his tail between his legs."

The sound of running anklets led him to her.

Suganthi. The Hoysala princess and daughter of Narasimhan III. She looked at Rajarajan from behind a pillar and continued hurling taunts at him. But instead of getting angry, Rajarajan started smiling. He chased Suganthi down and held her hostage, pinning her hands behind her back.

"Yes, that's how a coward will behave. Raju the coward," she cried and tried to free herself.

They looked at each other and started laughing. Childhood friends, they had been close since the time they used to attend school and games together. As children, they had spent practically all their time together. Theirs was the kind of friendship that can be taken for granted. And now, she had grown up to be a smart and inquisitive young woman.

"You bloody fool! Why did you blindly rush into battle? You know that's why you lost."

"Yes, I know. What would *you* have done, Suganthi?"

"I would have waited. I would have planned. I would have teased Sundara Pandyan out, somehow. I would have ensured victory, my coward prince!"

"Easier said than done, girl."

"You attacked with just 100 soldiers and allowed yourself to be surrounded. Didn't we learn to watch our back? Didn't we learn to look before we leap? Don't be a male chauvinist now and deny all this, just because I am saying it! You are the future of the Cholas."

She then went on to draw out her plan and explain how she would have analysed the situation and attacked the Pandyan forces. Rajarajan was flabbergasted! His little Suganthi had become a warrior strategist! He thought, "This is what I am missing. A partner with a head that's cooler than mine. Somebody who knows how to keep me in check. And someone who has my best interests at heart."

A week later, Narasimhan called for young Rajarajan. Why did the king take a whole week, Rajan thought, but he knew the answer. Why would Narasimhan support him? What's there to gain from helping an exiled prince who was on the run?

Alliance as the Way Forward

When Rajan was presented before Narasimhan, he took the elder's blessings. He then asked for permission to speak.

"Sire, let me paint a picture. Of a time when you are the lord of practically all the regions south of the Vindhyas. The Hoysalas, Cholas, Pandyas and some parts of the Pallava regions - all yours. The length and breadth of this great region pays obeisance to you and your progeny. You rule over a grand empire with vassals, chieftains and a vast army."

"You are a great storyteller, young man. But what's the purpose of this dream-mapping?"

"Sire, I came here to ask for your army. I am standing here now, asking for your daughter's hand. You know she and I are good friends. And in the last week, I have also realised what a great queen, strategist and commander she will make. With your blessings and her consent, I would like to marry her. We shall strengthen the bond between the Hoysalas and the Cholas. Together, we will weed out our common enemy, the Pandyas.

Imagine, Sire. Your grandson will be the king of this colossal empire. He may even rule the world!"

A cool-headed Rajan was a lot better than a hotheaded one. He knew his objective, but was also clear that he had to appeal to emotion.

What better way than marriage to seal an alliance between two kingdoms!

Rajan returned home with a strong partner, the Hoysala king's blessings and a large army.

* * *

> **INTERPRETATION**
>
> - We need to know the desires and aspirations of those we seek to have an alliance with.
>
> - What's in it for them? This needs to be answered clearly, as vividly as painting a picture.
>
> - Sometimes, solitary thinking helps us gain clarity of objectives and actions.
>
> - Wisdom comes in many shapes and forms. Listen and take it in.

MOOVENDHAR: A Question of Alliances

Rita: How can we enter a market without any connections?

JK: You look for partnerships — someone who can make the connections. Or ally with a company and use their network. Piggyback.

Rita: What's in it for them? Why should they do it?

JK: You've got something they want. They've got something you need.

Take the two-wheeler market in India.

The Japanese companies had the technology, R&D and experience in manufacturing world-class two-wheelers. The Indian firms knew the Indian market, and had a strong distribution base, and the ability to service and maintain the bikes. What happened, as a result?

Kawasaki joined hands with Bajaj.

Kinetic married Honda.

TVS entered into matrimony with Suzuki.

But, of course, all partnerships are time-bound. They reach an expiry date at some point of time. "What's in it for me?" has to be clear to all the parties concerned.

We have to think beyond the current wants, and look at future aspirations, as well. I can partner now. But in the process, am I creating a future competitor?

How do I weigh the merits of this alliance? What are the checks and balances?

The alliance between Japanese and Indian firms worked for many years. But after that, some Japanese firms quit the Indian market, while others entered the Indian market on their own. Yet others have taken a majority stake in their respective joint ventures.

Anu: I want more B2B alliances, and retail partners or franchises for my food business.

What would they want?

Rita: Hey! They will regularly need something to pique the interest of their customers. Some may want to white-label or co-brand, to access your creativity in new food combinations.

Gokul: My company needs pan-Indian reach, and we need partners with such a reach to help us hire locally, across regions. Attrition is an issue, and so is finding quality talent. If I pick the right vendor, would it be a partnership or a mere client-vendor relationship?

JK: If hiring is critical, invest in a partnership, Gokul. It is an alliance worth considering, looking at the long-term need and growth prospects.

Rita: My need is clear. I need to enter Germany. I need to look for market-entry partners and consultants. I also need to see if there is the possibility of an alliance with a German association. Or, I should create one locally.

JK: You have to be ready to give something, so as to get something. There's always a cost associated. You pay now or later. There are no free lunches here, folks. Look for alliances in logistics, marketing, human resources/people, product distribution or any other aspect of business, including any outlier alliance you can think of.

I'll give you an example. GoFloaters studied the daily work routine of field salespeople and came up with an interesting insight. Salespeople usually have some spare time between meetings, but are forced to spend it unproductively at roadside tea shops. Wouldn't it be great if they have a nice place to sit and work from, while they wait for their next meeting?

Shyam Sundar Nagarajan, Co-Founder of GoFloaters, tied up with cafes across Chennai and made an offer to companies: accessible workspaces in multiple localities for their field staff. Their salespeople could walk into the vetted cafes and spend their time working. They could prepare for their upcoming meetings.

It was a win for everybody: increased footfall for the cafes, increased productivity for the companies, and convenience and productivity for the salespeople. It was an alliance of cafes, companies and a binding agent (GoFloaters).

Marketing case in point

Energy drink brand Red Bull tied up with GoPro. Both brands target an audience that seeks thrills and wants to show off its adventurous spirit to the world. So they decided to join hands. Together, the brands have partnered with athletes and enthusiasts of extreme sports. Both now have a much stronger bond with their target audience, translating into a loyal tribe and revenue growth.

Chapter 4

What Will You Do Once Your Strategy is Known to the Enemy?

The quest for revenge is an excellent motivator for some.

Rajarajan, in his quest to avenge his father's death, attacked the Pandyas. After a resounding defeat and some soul-searching, he found an ally in Narasimhan III, the Hoysala king. Rajarajan married Narasimhan's daughter Suganthi. She was a great foil for him, bringing strategy and mental strength to the fold.

Rajarajan returned to the South, back to the erstwhile kingdom of the once-mighty Cholas. He returned with a significant portion of Narasimhan's army and the burning desire to exact vengeance upon Sundara Pandyan the murderer. He now had the confidence of a larger army. But his defeat at the hands of the Pandyas still rankled. Some thoughts and memories never go away. They keep returning to haunt us like ghosts, bringing anxiety and worry along. Rajarajan had to brush aside the memories of the defeat and trust the commanders of the Hoysala army.

What Will You Do Once Your Strategy is Known to the Enemy?

He now had two advantages, Suganthi and Agastyan. Suganthi was trained in war strategy, and kept him in balance. And Agastyan, Narasimhan's chief commander, was a wily, battle-scarred veteran with enormous experience. Narasimhan had asked Agastyan to accompany Rajarajan and assist him.

Agastyan preferred to remain in the shadows. Not much was known about him or his methods, except that he was revered. There was an aura about him, of seriousness and purpose. His expression was poker-faced, and his eyes never revealed anything. A disciplinarian, he relied on getting to know his opponents better. Always at the vanguard of every attack, he won the respect of his men. That brought in implicit and immediate obedience. His speed and agility defied his age. He demonstrated his prowess every day in the practice field with several weapons and simulated fights. Agastyan was the mentor Rajarajan had yearned for.

Considerable time was spent in the strategy tent, assessing internal strengths and weaknesses, and planning various defense and attack modes. Floor models of Sundara Pandyan's critical forts were made. A wall chart with the names of his commanders, their strengths and weaknesses was put up.

The Chola army was broken up into smaller units, and some men disguised themselves as villagers. Sundara Pandyan should not have an inkling of a big army moving towards him. Stealth and deception were at play. Agastyan knew what needed to be done. His methods were simple yet effective.

The men assembled at a pre-agreed location. The army took shape once again near a border fort. The troops encircled the fort and sent in a message asking the fort commander to surrender. When the answer was no, all communication and food supply routes to the fort were cut. Completely. After a week, the fort leader sent them a message asking for food for the elderly. Agastyan replied, asking the Pandya leader to send the elderly to the Chola tents, where they would be cared for. By the end of the second week, the fort leader had no choice but to give up the fort to save his people. The choices one is forced to make!

The bloodless takeover of the fort boosted the confidence of Rajarajan and his army.

They used the same strategy in the next couple of forts. By ensuring that no communication was leaked to fortifications and commanders further South, they had the power of surprise. There were able to completely snuff out all contact between the Pandya forts and the world outside.

These victories buoyed Rajarajan's spirits. He now wanted more. He pressed his commanders to ensure that more of his armies attacked Sundara's forces. More, more, more! Speed, speed, speed!

They reached the next inner perimeter of Sundara Pandya's region. The forces were split, with Agastyan leading one and Rajarajan, the other. Sundara had his region laid out in concentric circles, each ring defending the next inner ring — till the core.

Rajarajan and his army arrived at the next fort. This one was much bigger than the others. Encirclement, messages to the fort leader, and cutting out ingress and egress: they followed all this to the letter.

"Hey, we've been doing this for a while now. We know what we are doing," thought Rajarajan.

One week led to the next. And to the next. His supplies were running out and his men were getting tired of waiting. At the end of the fourth week, he received a message from Agastyan, advising him to give up the siege and join the other troops, who needed support in another area. Grudgingly, his army left the siege and made their way back to their new main base. Rajarajan's army was deflated. They moved slowly, wearily. It is hard to get over a loss.

After the initial wins, Rajarajan now had mud on his face again. He was fighting the superior forces of the Pandyas, who weren't giving up their forts like they had done earlier. The Cholas were a despondent lot.

And Rajarajan was a very worried man, once more. A worried man with a borrowed army!

What could he do?

"I did everything just like what we did earlier. And yet, why did we lose now?"

Rajarajan and his walking, meditative introspection — asking himself tough questions.

He reached the camp and went straight to Agastya's tent. Agastya's section of the army had captured two more forts in the meantime. Given Agastya's age, experience and respect for people around him, Rajarajan had no hesitation in asking him questions about the loss.

"Commander, why did I lose?"

"Sire, a strategy is useful only as long as it is a secret. We should never under-estimate the enemy. They have their spies and communication methods, which will continue to operate, regardless of the siege.

We have captured so many of their forts in the last few months. The news must have reached Sundara Pandyan. The forts that I captured had started digging tunnels to ensure a flow of supplies and information. It so happened that we arrived *before* this work could be completed; so they had to give it up. Your fort, though, was bigger and farther into the Pandya kingdom. And it had a mini lake inside. I am sure they had built many tunnels and even had a stockpile of food inside the fort."

What Will You Do Once Your Strategy is Known to the Enemy?

"Hmm...so what should we do?"

"Adapt. Now that this fort-encirclement strategy is known to them, all their other forts will be better prepared. We need to think of new methods. We will."

"So do we attack now?"

"Now, Sire, you will sleep and recharge! A fresh mind and body are required to formulate effective strategies."

* * *

INTERPRETATION

- Does your marketing plan talk about your strategy — for attack and defense?

- A strategy needs to adapt to the enemy. By using the same methods again and again, you are exposing yourself to losses.

- A leader must trust his commanders and allow them to do the job they are best suited for.

- Prepare for victory and defeat, gain and loss. A victory is just around the corner. So is a defeat.

- Surrender is not defeat. When the enemy is much stronger, flee and plan for an attack later — perhaps an indirect attack.

- Bloodless victories are that much sweeter. Only a capable leader is smart enough to plan for them. Mediocre leaders crave blood, and let vanity get in their way.

MOOVENDHAR: Pricing, Defense and Attack

Gokul: Pricing. This is a crucial factor in our winning and losing accounts. What can I do to build a strong defense base?

Rita: Why is pricing so vital that you have to hide it? Our pricing is right there on our website. We are quite open about it.

Anu: Hey, it's the same with me! My clients need to know my rates, at least my rack rates. And my competition gets to know it, soon after.

JK: Is price the only competitive factor?

Are you selling a commodity without any defining features?

Have you allowed yourself to be defined by just one parameter — price?

If you fight the price war, it will be a fight to the bottom. It is necessary to have penetration pricing for some of your offerings, especially new ones. But to make price your sole point of difference and your sole component of strategy will prove fatal. Reducing price is not a tactic to be used all the time and without thought of the consequences.

Remember, some corporate spies keep track of competition. That's a business in itself. You are being watched all the time, so to speak. I don't want to sound like we are in a spy movie, but isn't that the reality? Your resources are being interviewed by competition, either to poach them or to find out more about your strategies. You do the same, don't you?

Know as much as you can about your client and then add significant value to them. Provide them so much value that they will think hard about moving to someone else. Focus on making them succeed in their roles and business with the help of your offerings: this will ensure a bigger and better defense for you. Relationship-building: isn't that is the catchphrase, you youngsters?

Now you may think, what if my competitor gets to know my strategy? Let's take the case of Google.

Google's strategists must have thought long and hard, and must have decided to play for the long term. They released Android as an open-source operating system (OS). That increased the chance that many mobile manufacturers would use this OS. It allowed many developers to play with it and enhance it further. More people playing with the OS and more manufacturers using the system meant that many more consumers will spend time online on the Android OS.

Google owns and controls some part of the Android stack.

What Will You Do Once Your Strategy is Known to the Enemy?

Is it an attacking strategy or a defensive manoeuver?

By making the OS open source, Google, of course, lost revenue. This move also scuttled those relying on a license-based revenue approach. This was a defensive move by Google, for sure, when you consider Microsoft OS as their competition. On Apple, though, this was a frontal attack! Apple was on the rise, with a near-monopoly. It was also a closed box for many.

With an open-source OS like Android, Google ensured that the number of contributors to its attack force grew exponentially. It blew open the box, so to say.

So, three musketeers, what are you going to do now?

Marketing case in point

People wanted more.

More quality, more taste, more value.

Pizza Hut and Domino's were the top two pizza chains in the USA in the late 1980s. Price, service, quality: all three had to be good. But Papa John's decided to build its stronghold in "quality" to grab the consumer's mindspace.

It therefore created a differentiated value proposition: Better Ingredients, Better Pizza.

From being a small pizza delivery brand, Papa John's became the third largest chain in the USA within a decade.

Papa John's knew the strategy of the other pizza chains. But it noticed a change in the consumers' perceptions of the brands and found that a gap existed in the space of "quality". This was a slot it could quickly occupy. And it did!

It took the larger rivals a long time to respond to Papa John's quick growth.

Chapter 5

When Big Attacks Small: What to Do?

Have you seen a large cat attacking a smaller one?

As they sat around the campfire, Agastyan and Rajarajan analysed the actions of the past few months.

What worked, what did not? How they won some battles, and why they lost some. Questions, ideas, thoughts, discussions. A chat that had no end-time. Just the key people, the fire in front of them and the stars, above. The wind whistling past, rekindling dying embers and re-igniting conversations.

Agastyan asking Rajarajan,

"Have you seen a large cat attacking a smaller one?"

"Yes, I have."

"What did you observe?"

"The larger one tried to use force. It tried to jump on the little one and swat it to the ground. Always trying to use its superior strength and at times, its height, to its advantage. Always using might".

"What did the little cat do?"

"It tried to survive every attack. Bending, jumping, moving back, rolling over. The little one tried to find a nook or cranny to hide in. It used the bushes, the trees, the shrubs and every other defense it could find. It used small spaces that the large one couldn't get into."

"And...?"

"When the large cat got stuck in the small entrance of a hole, the little one attacked its face with everything it had. Of course, I did not see this happen, but I noticed the larger cat's bloodied face when it pulled itself out of the mouth of the hole. Ultimately, it gave up the fight. Completely."

"So what did you learn from this?"

"We need to have different strategies for different enemies, and use the natural environment around us to our advantage."

"So, now that we are on the verge of facing a rather large army, what should we do?"

Agastyan let this question hang in the air. He then got up, patted Rajarajan on his shoulder and went to bed. Rajarajan kept staring at the red-hot coals in front of him. Sometimes, answers are provided. But sometimes, only a question is asked; we need to find the answers ourselves.

When Big Attacks Small: What to Do?

The next morning, Rajarajan walked up to Agastya and laid out his plan to attack Manickam's forces, which had camped nearby. Manickam was a Pandya commander.

War was afoot.

Rajarajan's army was split into four platoons, each one heading in a different direction with specific instructions. The orders were clear, and Agastyan ensured that the commanders and the soldiers knew what was expected of them. Each platoon targeted a particular (and different) portion of the enemy's vast army.

One platoon hid in the supply pathway and ensured that none of the supplies reached the waiting Pandyan army. Instead, the supplies were routed to the Chola base camp. This was done on all possible routes.

Another platoon consisted of commandos trained in hand-to-hand combat. They unleashed lightning attacks at the younger, less experienced soldiers of the enemy. These professionals would sneak into and out of the enemy camp. In, kill, out — before the enemy even realised what was happening.

A third attack from the rear ensued. A Chola platoon sprinkled oil all over the place and lit fires. The earth would be scorching hot for another few days. There was no place now for the enemy to retreat to. They were in despair. Anxiety made them yearn for some action, to get back at the Cholas.

The fourth Chola platoon took a different tack. It provoked the Pandya army. Attacked slowly and moved back. When they did this for the third time, the frustrated Pandya forces gave chase. All the way into the ambush laid for them. By this time, the other three Chola platoons had converged at that point to form a united front against the Pandyas.

Arrows were let loose. Manickam and his men died, the same way Rajarajan's father had died.

Each Chola platoon targeted a specific area of the enemy camp.

The small cat used its strengths and the terrain to hit at the big cat's limitations.

"Attacking one body part at a time. Death by a thousand cuts. Good learning and implementation, Sire," praised Agastyan.

Rajarajan smiled. The best learning is when you are prodded in the right direction but find the solution yourself.

Now, there was just one more bastion to break, one big war to fight.

* * *

INTERPRETATION

- Use what you have — in and around you.

- Your strategy depends on what you have and what your enemy has.

- Use the advantages of your size to determine your attack strategy.

- Divide and rule.

- Attack one part or aspect at a time, whether it is war or a marketing problem.

MOOVENDHAR: Business Wars and Preparation

JK: In business and war, you can never be complacent. Never. You did sign up to keep running. Sometimes you have to run fast, at other times, jog. Walk, trot, canter, gallop. You have to do it all.

Anu: I am a small company. The prospect of a biggie entering my space is a constant worry.

JK: Ok. So what are you doing about it? If a biggie should come in, what will you do? Map it out and do it now!

They *will* come in. Plan for the scenarios and draw them into a situation that *you* control!

Anu, you also have to note that solo entrepreneurs and those you consider to be smaller will attack you. They will copy your business model and go behind the same clients, with a lower price as their only differentiator. "My product is similar to Anu's products but 25% cheaper!"

And what about someone who is of the same size as you?

What is your strategy for someone smaller, someone of the same size, and someone bigger than you?

A strategy to defend your turf and your clients!

This holds true for all of you. Plan for all scenarios, until you get hit by something you haven't planned for. And when that happens, jump back up and learn again.

To invert a line from the film "Runaway Jury",

"You've got to a bit more mouse and a bit less cat!"

Marketing case in point

Amazon and Flipkart have been aggressively expanding in India, and raining deals and discounts on the consumer. Neighbourhood grocery stores are facing immense pricing and inventory pressure from these behemoths.

But they, the Davids, are fighting back with the advantages of their (small) size. They are leveraging what they have built over years — customer relationships. Many local stores have personalised their service, expanded their inventory and started delivering products to the customers' doorsteps. They have embraced Whatsapp to take orders, and Google Pay or PayTm to accept payments. In some places, local stores have banded together to purchase products in bulk at a lower price and pass on the price benefit to their customers.

So, while the mighty e-commerce companies are very much around, the local grocery stores are guarding their territory very well!

Chapter 6

A Cornered Tiger is Most Dangerous

What choice did we have?

There was no retreat and no surrender.

Kill or be killed.

We chose...

Kuberan was Agastya's pet soldier. This young strapping officer wasn't perfect, but he was learning fast. He wanted action, and he wanted to lead an attack.

Hunger is always good, but is it the right time to attack? How will one know without trying?

They were somewhere between Uraiyur and Thanjavur, making their way towards Sundara Pandyan's main camp. The villages they crossed sang paeans of their local boy, Sullaan.

Sullaan the brave, the mighty, the future of the Pandyan army. Sullaan was the son of Velan, the legendary Pandyan commander. Songs of his valour were sung around the campfire; his strategies, his bravery and his loyalty to Sundara Pandyan were strung together in verses and set to tune. Village after village spoke about him.

At long last, they came to a fort being held by the man himself! Rajarajan asked Kuberan to lead the charge against Sullaan.

"This is your charge to lead. Pick your men and form your strategy. Go, bring me that fort!"

Kuberan was charged up. He organised a platoon. They staked out Sullaan's fort and figured out the number of people inside. Kuberan resorted to their usual strategy of encirclement. He knew though that this would not be enough. An extended siege would drain his men and resources. What could he do to draw Sullaan out?

He sent Sullaan a letter.

"Sullaan, I am Captain Kuberan from Rajarajan's army.

I have heard a lot about you. You and I are of the same age. From what I have heard, I respect your valour and achievements.

This is an opportunity for us to battle it out. A fight to decide which one of us is better. To decide whose songs will continue to play in the long wintry nights. I invite you to enter the battlefield, and fight my men and me.

I promise you that the people of your kingdom will be safe from any harm. It's just you, me and our men — a fight to the finish.

If you accept my challenge, you will find me waiting on the battlefield in front of your fort at sunrise tomorrow.

For Valour, For Victory.

Kuberan."

The sun was up bright and early, the next morning. The rays started melting the dewdrops on the leaves and grass. Kuberan's men were standing in formation, looking at the gates of the fort. The gates opened, and Sullaan and his men came out. They took the defensive formation, and both sides assessed each other. A long pregnant silence filled the area, like the lull before a storm. Both sides were ready and itching to get at each other.

Drums started rolling, and the playing of the bugle signalled the start of the battle.

Foot soldiers rushed forward to attack one another. They were followed by the horsemen. Kuberan and Sullaan stood eyeing each other. The battle peaked, with both sides equally poised and effective. At the right time, Kuberan blew his conch, and two smaller sections of his army entered the battlefield from either side. Sullaan and his forces were caught in a pincer grip! They could not retreat into the fort. They had no way out.

The scales had tilted. Kuberan had picked a war formation from the times of the Mahabharata. He had some of his foot soldiers lie on the ground on either side of the battlefield, hiding, awaiting his signal to attack the Pandyas.

Finally, it was 100 of Kuberan's men against 10 of Sullaan's. Sullaan and his men were surrounded. Their death and Kuberan's victory was certain.

In war and life, there are moments like these, when time stands still. When things move in slow-motion.

It was such a moment on the battlefield now.

Sullaan and his men stood in a tight circle, their backs to one another. They were circling around, swords and spears at the ready. Surrounding them were Kuberan's men, waiting for Sullaan to drop his sword and concede defeat.

A roaring war cry roused them all. Sullaan's yell held a specific connotation, a key message. It was a trigger for his men to not give up, to fight till their last breath. It was a counter-attack — to death. They attacked the Chola men around them with a wave of anger and energy not seen before. Kuberan's men were taken aback.

A Cornered Tiger is Most Dangerous

Standing with his men in a circle, Sullaan forced Kuberan's men to break their formation. This meant that they had to attack in a ring as well. So the number of people attacking at the same time was reduced. Sullaan and his men wreaked havoc. The confidence of Kuberan's men was shattered as they kept losing men.

It was a numbers game, though. And Sullaan did not have the numbers.

One by one, his men fell. Until only two of them remained, one being Sullaan. It was way past afternoon, and both sides were terribly tired. The remaining two Pandya men also fell. They were still alive, though, when they were brought into Rajarajan's camp.

Kuberan had his victory, but at a significant loss. After Sullaan and his man were tended to, they were brought before Rajarajan and Agastyan.

Kuberan could not control himself. He asked Sullaan.

"Why? Why?"

Sullaan replied, *"What choice did we have?*

There was no retreat and no surrender.

Kill or be killed.

We chose..."

Sullaan succumbed to his injuries the following day. A victor who chose his way of life. And death.

Some victories leave a bitter taste.

The following night, Agastyan saw Kuberan ruminating, gazing at the fire. Placing a hand on his shoulder, he said:

"The enemy who has nothing to fear is the most dangerous enemy. A cornered tiger will do anything to escape.

* * *

INTERPRETATION

- Kuberan had an advantage, yet he squandered it. He allowed Sullaan to dictate his attack formation. Instead of breaking the Pandya ranks and drawing them out, Kuberan encircled them and restricted the number of attacks that could be made simultaneously.

- Sometimes, one must step back even when in front, in order to advance faster and farther.

MOOVENDHAR: An "Almost Victory"

Gokul: We had it in the bag. Almost. Only to find out that we had lost it. It was as if our competition knew our weak point and pulled the rug from under our feet. It took the wind off my team's sails. It was in our grasp; we had the celebrations planned. And then...

JK: Haven't you heard the story of the marathon runner who was leading for most of the race? He was way ahead of the field, and could see the winning line as he entered the stadium for the finishing loop. His coach was encouraging him from the stands.

It was the last stretch; this race was almost his. Fifty meters from the finish line, he raised his hands in victory and started to blow air kisses to the crowd. His coach was frantically signalling to him to move faster. But our man wanted to revel in the moment. With twenty five meters to go, he heard a sound behind him. In the second it took for him to turn his head and look back, a wiry, hungry competitor sped up and overtook him — and won the race!

Cross the winning line and *then* celebrate. Remember, your competition is watching, and waiting for the right time to overtake you. And the right time comes when you are complacent, assuming that the race is yours!

Gokul: But you can't keep running all the time and looking behind your shoulder!

JK: We have to. This is the game we are in. The play we chose. So we might as well do it well.

Rita: So do we keep running a marathon?

JK: Not necessarily. The terrain and the competition define your moves. When you don't know much about the territory you will play in, you spend more time in researching it. Jog slowly.

In familiar terrain, you decide when to speed up and when to stop.

At specific moments though, stop, breathe and analyse. Is this race worth fighting? If yes, fight it well, mapping out the environment, the territory, the attack, the escape routes, etc.

But when your competition is cornered, they will react in unpredictable ways. Be ready for that, too.

In your quest for growth, buoyed by your initial success, you tend to move ahead full-steam. But at times, you need to step back, make space and then move forward again with renewed vigour.

Marketing case in point

Maggi noodles. Comfort food. *Soul* food. For millions.

In 2015, Maggi was banned by the Indian Government for containing unacceptable levels of MSG and on the suspicion that it contained lead. Within days, it was removed from shop shelves across the country. Gone. The brand simply vanished!

For the next five months, the brand's fans tried out other noodle brands, only to give up and pine for their favourite Maggi.

When Maggi returned (after cleaning up its act), it did so with a vengeance. It started advertising across media, with the message that it was safe to eat, had always been so.

The communication was directed at Maggi loyalists, of whom there are millions in India. At the core of the communication was the nostalgia associated with Maggi noodles: the special moments when people gorged on those noodles.

The campaign got a rousing response from consumers. The brand's Facebook feed was flooded with likes, comments, shares and even recipes. And stories of how Maggi was an important part of their life.

Maggi was cornered, but it fought back with everything it had —using nostalgia and emotional connect.

Chapter 7

Strategy is Grammar, O Marketer

"We cannot camp here!"

Flush from the recent victory against Sullaan, Rajarajan and his army were ready for the final thrust: the goal that had propelled all his action until now. The reason his men chose to follow him. The path to this day had been tumultuous, with several wins and setbacks. Rajarajan, under the tutelage of the senior commander Agastyan, had learnt a lot. It looked as if learning was going to be a lifelong exercise.

"We cannot camp here!" said Agastyan.

Why not?

"Because the land here is intractable. It is not suitable for defence of any kind. We will easily fall prey, even to a small force. We need to keep moving towards Mahendramangalam, where Sundara Pandyan is congregating all his forces."

"So we remain on the move? Isn't that dangerous? Won't our men get tired?"

"Yes and no."

Suganthi, Rajarajan's wife and Agastyan's goddaughter, came to their preparatory camp to wish them before the final onslaught. She joined their strategy discussion.

"We need to be on the move. Sundara Pandyan should not know when exactly we will reach his camp. But we need our men to be fresh, too. That is quite a conundrum."

Suganthi, a trained war strategist, put forth her suggestions. Men in those times, at least some of them, listened to sound advice, regardless of who it came from. We need more such men today.

Finally, a plan was agreed upon and put in motion.

Agastyan took one half of the army and moved in a roundabout manner towards the one key fort that stood between them and Sundara Pandyan's camp. Rajarajan lead the other half directly towards the enemy base.

Agastyan studied the fort that Velan, a Pandyan chieftain, was commanding. He staked it out for a couple of days and then encircled it. Velan was familiar with this strategy. The Chola camp stayed in place for one whole week. The men and their cooking fires let Velan know that a long siege was at hand. Firewood was being stockpiled outside the fort. Soldiers moved in and out of the Chola tents. Some walked around the fort and set up a rear-guard action base. Velan and his men kept vigil, and were ready, should Agastya's strategy change and they rush into an attack.

Rajarajan's forces, though, were visibly tired and were dragging their feet. It looked like months of battle and marching had hit them hard. Had the men hit their wall, the invisible wall that puts paid to all aspirations and pushes us to just lie down and sleep? Rajarajan urged them to continue, using encouraging words, taunts and orders. His men complied. But progress was slow. Is this the army that was going to defeat Sundara Pandyan?

Rajarajan ensured that his men got extra rations. He stood by the campfire and gave a rousing speech. A speech that evoked the valour and feats of the Chola dynasty, their commanders and soldiers. Stories of training with his blood brothers, and how Vikraman gave up his life for the larger cause. His speech charged up every single Chola soldier!

In his fort, Sundara Pandyan was smiling. But he was also worried. Every time there was some good news, his instincts kicked in. He was a smart king who knew how wily his enemies could be. The report he got was that Velan was holding his fort. Rajarajan was advancing slowly, and it would take his army at least three more days to come into Sundara's zone. Three days, during which they would not find a suitable place to camp at night. Sundara Pandyan had chosen

Mahendramangalam strategically. He ensured that his well-trained forces remained alert. It was now a game of waiting. To let the mouse come into his trap. Three more days, and he would forever eliminate the scourge — the Cholas — from the face of the earth. Three long days.

The morning of the second day, as Sundara's camp was slowly awakening, his soliders were roused by a cry. Their base was under attack! "Assassins have entered our camp and are slitting the throats of our soldiers!" was the cry from one of the Pandya soldiers. It was the sentries who had been killed. The men who were supposed to guard the fort and raise the alarm had been eliminated. One soldier, who had walked to the periphery for his morning ablutions, noticed a dead sentry and screamed. Right after that cry of terror, he joined the dead sentry on the ground as an arrow pierced his throat. But he had managed to raise the alarm before he fell.

The Pandya soldiers scrambled to get their weaponry and get into formation. Sleep hangover, mixed with confusion, meant that there was little cohesion in their actions. The soldiers had trained well, but not for the scenario of a surprise early morning attack.

Rajarajan's army stormed into the camp and started attacking Sundara's army. There was a significant obstacle to the South of the Pandyan camp. So Rajarajan attacked from the East. It was mayhem for a while, but Sundara's army got their wits together. A fightback ensued. Trained Pandyan soldiers got over their stupor and started getting their act in place. Their collective muscle memory was returning. Rajarajan's archers, though, knew who to target. They ensured that the key leaders in Sundara's army were felled first. This led to confusion in the Pandya ranks. The Cholas' goal was to disturb the Pandyas' mental equilibrium, and they succeeded in doing so.

Rajarajan's aide raised the Chola flag and blew the bugle: the signal for Agastyan and his forces to join the battle. They attacked from the West. Sundara's men were shocked by this new army joining the enemy. To the North, there was only one small path through which they could escape. In the heat of the battle, mentally disturbed and having seen one more army attack them, a few soldiers from Sundara's army made a break for it. They rushed to the narrow path to escape. More of their fellow soldiers followed. And soon, it was a stampede.

Sundara looked at this running tribe and grimaced. What a shame!

The escaping soldiers met the arrows from the Chola archers, who were waiting for this very moment. This was going to be a rout.

Sundara Pandyan knew that his game was up. He was surrounded, but he continued to resist.

Rajarajan went up to him and invited him to a swordfight. It was a sight to behold. All fights and skirmishes around them stopped as the other men watched the two leaders fight. The advantage ebbed and flowed each way, until finally, the youth and energy of his enemy got the better of Sundara.

Rajarajan, after a long wait, avenged the death of his father.

He was supposed to feel elated. Instead, he felt hollow inside. He could not put his finger on the reason, but he felt sad. He walked away from the battlefield, lost in thought. He wondered why he wasn't feeling satisfied even after achieving his objective!

* * *

The night when they had been strategising, Suganthi came up with a plan to split the Chola army to deceive Sundara Pandyan about the Chola army's size.

Rajarajan had to ensure that his men acted tired and wobbly, to give the impression that they were spent. This was part of the ploy. During the night, though, his men moved forward in double-quick time to reach Sundara's camp much earlier — taking them by surprise.

Agastya's role was to seem to attack and capture Velan's fort. He made a big show of encircling the fort. But in fact, leaving behind a few men to keep up the pretense of a long siege, he took most of his army and side-stepped the fort altogether. When asked why, he said there was little to be gained from capturing the fort. "It will not provide us any significant advantage over Sundara Pandyan." At best, it would have been a distraction, making them lose some men and time. Instead, Agastya and his men walked around the fort and sped forth to join Rajarajan's unit at the right time and place.

Agastyan knew Rajarajan's state of mind. After everything was over, he went up to the Chola leader and said:

Strategy is grammar.

* * *

INTERPRETATION

When you know the framework, the rest of the tactics depend on the enemy's size and moves.

We need to be like water, Agastyan said. Water flows. It adapts to its immediate environment. It takes the shape of the vessel it is in. Changing shape and nature, finding gaps and crevices — it does whatever needs to be done.

* * *

Strategy is grammar.

One who understands grammar will mould himself and adapt his words to communicate well.

One who understands the strategy of war knows which moves and tactics to make, to win.

In today's world of marketing communication,

Strategy is grammar that defines who, why, what and when!

* * *

MOOVENDHAR: Fight the Right Fight, Well!

Anu: So should I fight every day?

JK: Fight, but only the right fights. If there is not much to be gained through an action, it is best to avoid it; no point doing it for minimal gain.

Gokul: How many scenarios do I plan for? And who should I attack or defend myself from?

JK: Doesn't Surf, the detergent brand, have many variations in its product mix? It does, to cater to different consumer segments, addressing the needs of each one of them. The core of the product could be the same, but its variants can be customised. The scenarios they planned for included some knowns and some unknowns. Despite that, did not a small, one person-driven Nirma knock them off the pedestal for a while?

Plan for all possible scenarios, especially for attacks from those you think will not or cannot attack you. At a time you think is impossible.

Rita: I have read that Netflix keeps testing its website, including its look and feel, constantly: A/B testing to ensure the best response. Isn't that preparing for an attack?

JK: Could be. It is also to stay in touch with the mood-swings and ever-changing tastes of their customers.

Let me narrate an episode I heard from Seth Godin.

Long before the age of Google and SEO, in one of his entrepreneurial ventures, Seth Godin realised that competition was constantly watching them. Not only watching, but also aping them. They kept checking his website for updates and new releases, and quickly developed the same: the solutions, use cases and sometimes, even the language.

This was getting out of hand. But Seth's company's website was public, and his prospects came to him through that. So what could he and his team do?

They decided to use the power of deception. They started thinking of zany features and initiatives, and posting them on their website. Plans that seemed far-fetched but necessary.

The competition caught on and spent quite many midnight hours trying to copy those features and initiatives.

All this while though, Seth's team had designed another website in stealth mode. Only their clients and key prospects could access it. Of course, this was a short- to mid-term move, but one that was necessary to divert the attention of pesky, plagiarising competitors!

Developing one website is easy. But handling *two* takes sleight of hand and a lot of planning. Seth's move could have gone either both way; for or against him. So it had to be monitored continuously and kept a secret. But his team carried it off.

So be on the move always. Be like water. Flow and adapt to the environment you are in. Be a river that flows through mountains, gorges and plains. At times, be like vapour and steam. And at other times, be as cold and hard as ice.

Marketing case in point

Netflix's goal in India was to be the premier web streaming channel. OTT was an emerging concept then. Since Netflix wanted more Indians to tune into it, it had to be top-of-mind for consumers, and the first port of call to watch movies and serials.

They used a variety of tactics to suit different viewer segments. They offered a 2-day free trial as a sampler. They forged unique partnerships — such as the one with Swiggy, a food delivery platform, to play trailers while customers waited for their orders. Also, Netflix invested significantly in ramping up original Indian content. This ensured a strong local connect with its target audience.

These moves paid off. Netflix steadily gained market share to become one of the top 3 OTT channels in India. Through all this, the brand's tongue-in-cheek, witty responses on social media kept the conversation alive among users, especially millennials.

SECTION 2

REVERSE REVENGE

Chapter 8

The Lull after the Storm

"Prepare for war!"

Rajarajan III returned to Uraiyur a victorious king. He had last visited the city when his father, Kulothunga Cholan III, had been the ruler. So much had changed since then.

Rajarajan had grown in strength and maturity over the last couple of years. He had found his consort Suganthi, his mentor Agastyan and the love of his soldiers.

Now, a bigger — and different — challenge awaited him: to learn the ropes of being a good ruler and get used to the lull after the war storm.

Could the strategies of war be used in ruling a kingdom during peacetime? He was about to find out.

Rajaraja Cholan III's coronation was a grand affair. His people rejoiced. Neighbouring kings and princes arrived, bearing gifts. Physical gifts, and the gift of friendship and alliance.

The new king got busy, familiarising himself with the affairs of the state. His focus was on revenues, distribution and the various other issues brought to his palace. This was a new set of problems, which had to be analysed through a different lens. And the solutions had to not just *be* equitable, but also be *perceived* as such. Reputation is built step by step.

His soldiers, who had been on battle fields for close to two years, were having adjustment issues. Drunken brawls and fights within families were being reported frequently. Once-vaunted soldiers were now on the verge of being disrespected by the populace. A fall from grace wasn't far ahead. When this matter came up to Rajarajan, he wondered what the core of the problem could be.

He reached out to Agastyan. Agastyan had been loaned to Rajarajan as a war commander by the Hoysala king Narasimhan III. When the war was over, he had returned to the Hoysala kingdom despite several requests from Rajarajan to stay back. But now, he was back in Uraiyur as a "coach on demand".

Agastyan took a week to walk around the kingdom. He took mental notes and observed all that was happening. Some soldiers recognised him and walked up to him for a chat. He camped overnight in villages. Campfire connections continued as he received direct feedback on the state of the nation, the issues and people's individual concerns.

The Lull after the Storm

"Prepare them for war!" said Agastyan upon his return to Rajarajan's palace.

"Why? It has been but a year since we returned from a big war!" said Rajarajan.

"Yes. But they have to prepare for war again. A different one. The men need a routine. They need something to channel their energies into. On the battlefield, you channeled their anger towards the enemy. They knew what they had to do. There was a common purpose and goal.

When they woke up every morning, what they did during the day, how they conducted themselves — everything was clear. But returning to civilian life, they have a lot of time on hand, and little to do. Their idle minds have become the devil's workshop. Some of them have resorted to teasing and tormenting other people. Others have taken to alcohol. A few just laze around, adding inches to their waistline. In their civilian avatars, these men have become a drag on the kingdom.

So now, we need to funnel their energy towards something they know well. Let's prepare them for war and sharpen their skills."

And so, the soliders were recalled, and training started. No additional information was given, but a routine was set. A routine they had to strictly adhere to. Most of them returned to the training camps and resumed sharpening their fighting skills. Those who could not fight were rounded up and trained for civilian jobs — farming, blacksmithing, carpentry, armament-making and so on. Some of them were directed to safeguard the kingdom's borders and quell minor rebellions. Some others became war scouts, identifying and recruiting young talent from within the kingdom.

All in all, the men were so tired from working their beat from dawn to dusk, that they had neither the time nor the interest to trouble anybody. Moreover, even a whiff of alcohol coming from them meant heavy punishment.

Within three months, all their behavioural issues resolved themselves.

His job completed, Agastyan took leave of Rajarajan. But only after giving him one last piece of advice.

"In peace, prepare for war. In war, prepare for peace."

* * *

The Lull after the Storm

INTERPRETATION

- Your team needs a specific purpose at all times; a goal to work towards. Idling isn't good for your business.

- When your company is on the warpath (read, implementing a strategy or campaigning for something specific), your team is fully focussed on doing the assigned tasks well. But during down-time, ensure that you channel their energies towards some other gainful purpose.

MOOVENDHAR: A Relay Race for Muscle Memory

Rita: JK, you said I have to keep running. Wouldn't that tire me and my team out?

Gokul: My question, too!

JK: You have seen a relay race. One person in the team starts the race. She finishes one lap and passes the baton to the next runner, who runs a lap and passes the baton on to another runner and so on, until the last person finishes the race. Each person is selected for a specific role: the starter, the stabilizer and the finisher. At any point of time, there is always someone running, someone planning, and many people supporting and cheering.

When you channel your team's energy in a single direction, it keeps you all engaged in achieving a shared objective.

Anu: How do I interpret this baton-passing in a startup like mine or in a company like Gokul's, which has stabilised?

JK: As we saw in the story, in peace, prepare for war; in war, prepare for peace.

When you are fighting for market share in one territory, you will be defending another territory. After one victory, if you lie back thinking you have won, another defeat will invariably be around the corner. Or, when you are fighting in one market, there could be peace in another market.

When things appear stable, plan for instability. When you think you have won market share, be ready for competition from new and established players. Prepare for competition's counter-attack. Be prepared for action, and an equal and opposite reaction.

Let us take training, for example. We train salespeople to sell well. We then let them be, thinking that the spike in sales will continue. But actually, the market keeps evolving, and therefore, we need to keep the training on. The medium of training may change; the effort and planning should not! A gentle nudge to encourage the self-starters and a hard push to goad those who want to rest on their laurels. Any which way, training has to be continuous. We need unsupervised, self-driven performers in a distributed working world.

As one team is running, other teams strategise, plan, work on new product development. Teams build muscle memory, so that every person knows what needs to be done when the time for action comes.

Marketing case in point

In its heydey, 3M encouraged every employee to spend up to 20% of their time on innovation. On finding the next big solution. On finding a product that could be patented. This ensured that the creative juices of the team kept flowing even during 'peacetime'. The employees felt empowered to pursue their ideas and try to commercialise them. When they were in this mode, they become their own bosses!

What can I do today? What can I try and succeed or fail in? Which new product can I research and develop? They kept asking themselves these questions, ensuring that there was always a buzz in the company.

Thanks to this approach, 3M, over the years, patented and commercialised scores of new products that added to their topline and bottom line.

Chapter 9

Winds of Change... Spark a Wildfire

"You've always been a greedy, selfish bastard.

Your whole world is just you, right?

Shame on you!"

Vira Someshwara was crowned king of the Hoysalas. What a long wait it had been for him! He had been waiting in the wings to take over from his father and implement his own grand plans for the kingdom. But his father, Narasimha II, took his sweet time to hand over the reins. He wanted Someshwara to be ready. Now, of course, with his declining health, the old king had to let his son ascend to the throne to ensure continuity.

Someshwara was deferential to his father, though he had his own plans. He felt that his father had spent so much time focusing outside the kingdom, that he hadn't grown their defenses. Also, he felt that the alliances his father had made were all in good faith, but did not make much business sense. The senior partner in an alliance must be paid, in cash or kind, he believed. Over the years, the Hoysalas had helped their Southern neighbours. But his father had waived off revenue and royalty collections from them, and this was hitting the Hoysalas hard. Someshwara had inherited a kingdom that was good only in name. Its finances needed serious and immediate repair.

Not just that. With Narasimha having focussed exclusively on the Tamil kingdoms of the South for a long time, Hoysala's Northern neighbours were acting up. Those on the other side of the Tungabhadra river crossed over and attacked his people at will.

Someshwara strengthened the defenses all around and conducted raids into enemy territory. He neutralised his enemies and placed his vassals to govern the regions, thereby expanding the Hoysala kingdom. As tax revenues and royalties started to come in, it gave him the confidence and additional income to plan further. Every new king had to prove himself to his people. Someshwara won the appreciation of his people, as he provided them more and reduced their taxes.

A niggling thought, though, remained. If those in the North could pay him royalty, why weren't the Southern allies doing so? Why weren't the Cholas, who the Hoysalas helped win a big war, paying them anything? Or the Pandyas, whose regions they helped the Cholas acquire? Some of the spoils from those

Winds of Change...Spark a Wildfire

victories should come to the Hoysalas by right. But he kept these thoughts to himself.

His sister Suganthi, wife of Rajarajan III, had come home to deliver her third child. She was a well-read military strategist, and took an active interest in all affairs of the State. She was now the queen of the Chola kingdom. It was her marriage to Rajarajan that sealed the alliance between the Hoysalas and the Cholas. Her son would take over the Chola throne when he was ready. The Chola-Hoysala bloodline will rule. But when she mentioned this to Someshwara casually, he felt a pang. Does this mean that my son will not rule this region, will not be the emperor of the entire South, he wondered.

Some conversations create a spark. And if a wind blows at the right time, that single spark can grow into a raging fire, consuming everyone in its vicinity. Someshwara's pang grew stronger by the day. "I can be the emperor of all the Southern lands and pass them on to *my* son," he thought. He consulted his ministers, who also felt that the Cholas must pay the Hoysalas royalty. After all, the Hoysalas had helped Rajarajan win his kingdom from the Pandyas. So he was a part of the Hoysala kingdom.

Someshwara did not talk to his sister about this. Instead, he sent Rajarajan an emissary, clearly stating his stance. He spoke of all the help that the Hoysalas had provided, without which Rajarajan would have been nothing. So taxes and royalty must be paid, he said.

Rajarajan read the letter and kept his own counsel for the night.

"My wife Suganthi is right there, with Someshwara. We are all part of the same family, after all. Then why did he write a letter like this? What's on his mind?" he wondered. He then wrote to his wife, asking for further details and encouraging her to have a word with her brother.

Suganthi was furious when she read her husband's letter. She rushed to Someshwara's chamber.

"You've always been a greedy, selfish bastard. Your whole world is just you, right? Shame on you!

Don't you realize that the Cholas are part of our family now? And I am the queen of their kingdom. What's got into you? Did you talk to father about it?"

Someshwara was silent. He looked at her and said,

"My son will be the emperor of the entire South. The Cholas would be nothing without our support. What the North pays us, the South must, too."

A tense silence continued as the siblings stared at each other. Suganthi knew her brother well. She knew that once his mind was set, it was difficult to change it. This time though, she was in direct conflict with him and his people, who were also *her* people! Family, people and allegiances will be put to the test soon.

There was a new king on the throne, and it was his ambition at play.

Suganthi's allegiance now lay with the Cholas. She knew both the kingdoms. More importantly, she knew her brother well. Well enough to know what his next move would be. He was relying on his council of ministers, more than on his commanders.

Alliance politics were going to change.

Conflicts were going to arise.

War was coming to the land again.

* * *

INTERPRETATION

Be ready.

The onus will shift from the likelihood of an enemy not attacking to one's own readiness for the attack.

Be ready. To defend and to attack.

MOOVENDHAR: Strategy

JK: What is the key to strategy?

Anu: Knowing what to do.

Gokul: Knowing what to do when.

Rita: Knowing what to when, how and with/for whom?

JK: Good. What is critical, though?

The three CEOs were silent.

JK: How well do you know yourself? What are your weaknesses and strengths?

Gokul: Come on, JK. That is a fundamental SWOT analysis!

JK: Yes, of course. But have you done it for yourself? In the recent past? Or ever at all?

Gokul: Umm...no.

JK: Well, the core of strategy comes from within: knowing oneself and one's company. A SWOT analysis, for sure. You know what we do, though. Once we know our weak points, we compare those with the strengths of our competition. We put ourselves down. We get into in self-deception, amplifying our own strengths and weaknesses!

We have to know ourselves well, and we have to compare apples with apples. Our strengths with those of our allies and competitors. And the same with our weaknesses.

A strategy is all about achieving our objectives and manoeuvering to achieve them. Planning and action. It is about mapping not just the *actions* of our competitors, but also their *aspirations*. As winds change, so do some people's minds. We need to be conscious of that, and feed that into our strategy and scenario-planning. The muscle memory we spoke about earlier applies to planning, as well. Yes, there will be a few unexpected things, but we need to anticipate most of them and have an action plan ready.

We focus on being busy, that we miss out on allocating the time and hard work needed to strategise. We need to know ourselves first, and then them.

As Sun Tzu said many centuries ago,

If you:

1. Know the enemy and know yourself, you need not fear the result of a hundred battles.

2. Know yourself but not the enemy, for every victory, there will also be a setback.

3. Know neither yourself nor the enemy, start digging your grave right away.

So Gokul, shall we do a SWOT analysis now?

Marketing case in point

Change was in the air. Indian consumers were becoming more conscious of the perils of junk food. They were keen to eat healthier. They wanted to cut down on products that used maida, like cakes and biscuits. It was a slow movement, but one that was enough to make a dent in the sales of Britannia's main product lines.

Quick to take note of this change, Britannia brought out a range of healthier biscuits and started promoting them aggressively. Named NutriChoice, this range included sugar-free biscuits, digestive crackers and other such options.

This helped the company two-fold. It helped it retain its existing customers and recruit erstwhile buyers of competition brands, as well.

Chapter 10

Short-Term Alliances for Long-Term Growth?

Someshwara was no kid. He had earned his stripes. When his sister left his palace in a huff, he knew what she was thinking. Cut from the same cloth, both siblings were equally smart and stubborn. Ambitious, too.

He had known that this day would come — when the family would be split. He had to answer to his father, but was thankful that his father did not interfere in the way he ruled the kingdom. Narasimha had allowed Someshwara to come into his own, and set his rules and ways of working. This was something Someshwara wanted to keep in mind when the time came for *his* son to take over — hopefully, as emperor of the entire South!

His army was ready. Agastyan, their ertwshile commander, had retired. He had been the one who had trained Someshwara and his new arch-rival, Rajarajan III. It was going to be a battle of equals. Someshwara wondered how he could tilt the balance towards himself.

He called his bunch of ministers and his war cabinet. His instructions were clear.

"We need to reign in all of the South, own this region. Within the next three years. What must be done? Plan now for all possible scenarios."

For the next ten days, his ministers put their heads together. They mapped all the neighbouring kingdoms, their allegiances and, more importantly, the needs and wants of each of those kingdoms. They mapped their neighbors' fears and discussed what had to be done to bring the neighbours on board. They detailed out and analysed several "what if" situations.

Plans, so essential to fall back upon, especially when one of them fails. One of the many things they had learnt from Agastyan, who continued to influence them even in his absence.

Someshwara was ready. He sent his spies all over the region to ascertain ground realities, which he then fed into his strategy. He sent for Maravarma Sundara Pandyan II, the son of Sundara Pandyan, who had been killed by Rajarajan III.

Maravarman was confused when he received Someshwara's letter. Someshwara, whose father had allied with the Cholas to kill Maravarman's father and defeat the Pandyas. And now, the same Someshwara wanted to meet Maravarman! Why?

Short-Term Alliances for Long-Term Growth?

Maravarman had no kingdom at the moment, but he consulted his band of advisors. He decided to travel to meet Someshwara. Curiosity definitely is a big motivator.

Arriving at Someshwara's palace, he was ushered in. Two ornate chairs were kept in the reception hall, both at the same level. There is so much in the unsaid that sends a clear message. **Equality. Respect. Connect.** Those were the words that resonated within Maravarman when he saw the chairs.

Someshwara welcomed him and invited him to have a seat. And then, asked him:

"Would you like to have your kingdom back? Would you like to bring back the Pandya rule in your region?"

Someshwara sure did not beat around the bush. He asked the question straight, evoking a nervous, cracking laugh from Maravarman. But when the Pandya prince studied Someshwara's serious expression, he realised that the Hoysala king meant business.

"Yes, of course."

"Are you ready to go to war again, to get it back?"

"Yes."

"Are you ready to do whatever it takes to resurrect your lineage?"

"Yes!"

"Then swear allegiance to me. You will consider me your emperor, and pay me a royalty in return for my continued support and protection. I will partner with you, share my army and help you get your kingdom back. The regional boundary between kingdoms will be redrawn and will be respected. Do you agree?"

Maravarman thought for a while. What did he have to lose?

"Yes, Sire. I promise you my loyalty. I accept your proposal."

Maravarman was invited to spend the next few days in the Hoysala palace to plan things before moving forward.

Someshwara had made his first move in the chess game of Southern supremacy.

* * *

INTERPRETATION

All alliances are based on needs and wants.

"What's in it for me?", "What's in it for them?" and "What's in it for us?" needs to be asked and answered. That is the basis of all negotiations and agreements. Know the desires, fears and aspirations of your neighbours and potential partners.

One who invests time in knowing all this will always be the victor.

MOOVENDHAR: Outlier Alliances

JK: We are back to discussing alliances. We spoke about winds of change. No partnership remains constant. There is always some change in the offing. The contact person in a company changes, the company gets acquired by another company, or a new division is formed — or closed.

Rita: So what? Do we always spy on allies, as well?

JK: Spying. Corporate espionage seems very James Bondish. I don't mean that. But at a more human level, we need to keep track of our stakeholders and everyone else in the ecosystem. You may choose not to do anything about the knowledge you gain this way. But you cannot stop the competitors from doing what they ought to do with the knowledge *they* have about you.

Everything is fair in love and war — and in corporate alliances.

Look at addressing the critical question, "What's in it for me?" Answer this for your client, your partner/vendor and all potential allies.

Go beyond traditional alliances that your competition and linear thinking can easily come up with. Use unconventional outlier thinking to connect random dots.

Surprise becomes a keyword. When you go with unthought-of combinations, it takes the world by surprise and gives you that bit of strategic advantage. A short-term point of differentiation that you can milk.

"What's in it for me, them and us?"

Marketing case in point

In its early days, Air Deccan, without the money, power or travel agent network that big airlines had, was fighting a tough battle. So it had to innovate. Its think tank came up with something very unconventional.

Who was their air service meant for? For the average Indian, who travelled by train but aspired to fly. Where did this average Indian live, and how did they communicate? How could Air Deccan reach them easily, all over India?

In 2007, India Post had a vast network which reached deep into Air Deccan's target segments. And so, the airline partnered with Indian Post to sell tickets in small towns and villages across India. The company piloted 500 internet-enabled post offices in Karnataka before expanding to other places. Each of these post offices became a ticket booking point for the airline. It would collect the money, hand over the ticket to the customer and take a commission from Air Deccan.

It was a win-win-win alliance. Convenience and accessibility for consumers, an additional revenue stream for India Post, and a pan-India distribution network of over 150,000 "ticketing agents" for Air Deccan!

Chapter 11

Stay on the Cutting Edge, Literally

"Do you still have the fight in you?"

That was the question Someshwara asked Maravarman over breakfast.

"Of course, yes. Why are you asking me this now?"

"Because I need to know. *You* need to know. You are a key ally, and an important part of my plans. Do you still have the fight in you? The desire, anger, skill and will?"

"Yes. How can I prove it to you?"

"Take 1000 of my men and show it to all of us."

"A 100 would do, Sire!"

And so began Maravarman Sundara Pandyan's quest for vengeance and the reclamation of the Pandya kingdom.

He left with his 100 men, and met Selvam and Singaram — his aides, his commanders. Selvam had trained with Maravarman's father, while Singaram had trained with him. Their fates were tied to his, by choice and by affection. They were pleased with the prospect of an alliance with the Hoysalas, but were bemused to hear the challenge they now faced. Selvam gently admonished Maravarman.

"When you are given 1000, you take 1000. You've let vanity get in your way. Now we have a taller mountain to climb. But we will."

It was obvious that they could not fight the Chola army with 100 soldiers. So what could Maravarman do to prove that he had fire in his belly?

"We need to make a statement," said Singaram vehemently.

"Yes, but without losing many men!" countered Selvam with a smile.

A statement that would help reunite the scattered Pandyan forces. A statement that would send Someshwara a reply and Rajarajan III, a clear message.

With a small force, they could move faster. They identified a slightly bigger enemy army on the border between the Hoysala and Chola kingdoms.

Taking a few soldiers along with him, Selvam staked out the enemy camp. He studied their location and the surrounding areas. Once he returned, their attacks began. It was a series of small, lightning strikes. One day, the horse riders would go in, attack the enemy camp and exit from the other side. Another day, a small group would attack the sentries and soldiers on the periphery and run back. This started happening consistently. The enemy was now aware of what was happening.

When the sixth such raid began, the enemy quickly jumped into an attack formation and gave chase. Surprised, Maravarman's men turned back, full speed. The Chola platoon chased them and started gaining on them. The path was clear, and the last soldier who was running away was visible to the Cholas. Their captain encouraged his men to move faster. All of them had eyes only for the scared soldiers running ahead of them.

Before they knew it, the entire Chola platoon was stuck in a quicksand, something they had been deliberately led into. Maravarman's raiders had mapped out this marshland and deliberately led the enemy into it. Sinking slowly, it was panic and chaos in the Chola ranks! When they were well and truly stuck, the Hoysala-Pandya soldiers returned. Their archers then finished the job the raiders had started.

A smaller Pandya force that had already encamped nearby swooped down and eliminated the remaining men who were guarding the Chola base.

With renewed vigour, Maravarman and his men had moved past the first hurdle.

Maravarman then chose to take on a Chola unit that was five times the size of his. Singaram went ahead to reconnoiter the enemy region, their base camp and the land. He knew they couldn't get lucky with their marshland tactic again. They would have to adapt their approach to this larger army and a different environment. Singaram was looking for chinks in the enemy's armour that they could leverage.

The Chola base camp was well-positioned, with 500 soldiers. It was a clearing in the forest, with trees all around. There was enough space between the camp and the trees to enable the Chola soliders to watch out for enemy movement. The sentries on duty were fresh and alert.

Maravarman paraded the 100 men in a mock attack. The Chola sentries were alarmed, and the whole camp was up. So then, Maravarman's men retreated and spread out. Birds started flying all around the base camp. Trees shook, and footsteps could be heard. The whispers started. Once whispers start, it is difficult to contain them. Small gangs of whispering men could be seen. "Oh, we have been surrounded! Did you see the trees shake, and all the birds fly away? It must be a huge army!" And so the word spread.

A strong wind began after some time. The shaking trees, this time due to the wind, were rattling the Chola soldiers. Maravarman's archers sent fire-tipped arrows into the Chola camp. Lit arrows aimed at the tents caused many small fires. The Chola men had to rush out. In the confusion, many more fell to the arrows. Even if they wanted to attack, they did not know where the enemy was.

The Chola leader realised what was happening and quickly disciplined his men into a defensive formation. There was noise all around, and a cyclone was kicking up tons of dust. Chaos prevailed.

When the dust cloud reached its peak, Maravarman's forces attacked. They were well prepared, having covered their eyes with a cloth, leaving only a slit to see through. They attacked the Cholas in a circular formation and broke their defense. The Cholas did not know the real size of their enemy. They *thought* it was a big army. Many Chola soldiers laid down their weapons and gave up the fight.

A hundred men won over five hundred with relative ease.

Earlier, Singaram had studied the wind and rain path, and had predicted a cyclone. A cyclone meant dust, which meant low visibility.

With two wins and the capture of two border regions, Maravarman Sundara Pandyan had more than proved himself. To his men and to Someshwara.

He chose to stay on the cutting edge of performance and victory.

* * *

INTERPRETATION

- Know the terrain well. What's your base? How strong is it? What is the base you are looking at capturing? What is it like?

- Read the local ecosystem well. Anticipate the changes that are in the offing, the cyclones that are brewing. See if you can use that to your advantage.

MOOVENDHAR: What You See is False!

Rita: I can relate to the story. Recently, we wanted to acqui-hire a company that was creating a lot of buzz in the market. From all that noise, we thought that the company was huge, with many clients. During due diligence, though, we found that it was just a small firm with a good marketing arm! We did acquire them, with their marketing arm being a key factor in our decision.

JK: What else can you relate this story to?

Gokul: When the chips are down, for the economy and the market, it is a good time to make a forward move. It's like the quote attributed to Baron Rothschild: "When there's blood on the streets, it's the time to buy." When the going is tough, like a storm or a recession, that will be the best time to attack and gain market share.

Anu: Use the power of deception to showcase a bigger, better army. From what Rita says, it is an awareness tactic, but a necessary one for small companies.

JK: Yes. Observe. Analyse. Act. You need to know the marketplace and ecosystem well. The better we know them, the better we can plan and execute. What are the customer's needs? What are the market conditions? What could be the cloak and dagger moves of the competition? It is like a chess game. We need to out-think and out-do. Consistently.

And Anu, regarding your earlier question, we need to hone our corporate espionage skills. We need to find out exactly what capabilities competition has. When the enemy is in sight, keep a lookout for other dangers that will come in.

There's a saying in Tamil:

"Kannaal paarpathum poi, kaadhaal kaetpadhum poi. Theera visaarippathey mei."

What you see is false.

What you hear is false.

What you investigate thoroughly and find out is the truth.

Staying on the cutting edge means thinking beyond competition and acting faster than them.

Marketing case in point

Car companies spent close to $60 million on advertisements during Super Bowl 2015 in the USA. But during the same period, Volvo increased sales of its XC60 model by 70% without spending a dime.

How?

Volvo encouraged the viewer of any car's TVC (television commercial) to tweet who they would like to give a Volvo to. All that the viewer had to do was tweet the name of the person with the hashtag #volvocontest, and that person could win a brand-new Volvo car.

Many people came to know about this campaign. TV host Jimmy Kimmel spoke about it, as did a lot of netizens. The moment viewers saw a car ad, they got busy tweeting #volvocontest. The campaign generated a very large number of responses across the USA.

Volvo ambushed its competitors and hijacked their viewers' attention. It effectively got them to focus on *its brand at the expense of competition*. This is known as The Greatest Interception ever!

Chapter 12

The Final Chapter

"It is time for you to avenge the death of your father."

Someshwara was pleased with Maravarman's show of strength. Capturing two regions and a fort, with only 100 soldiers. He had proven his hunger and his cunning. The irony was not lost on Maravarman. A few years ago, Rajarajan had been in the same position he was in now!

He was ready, and had planned his moves and counter moves. The much larger Hoysala army was now put at his disposal.

The Chola army was large but similar to the Hoysala force. After all, it was the Hoysalas who had trained and helped the Cholas reclaim their kingdom and rebuild their might!

How could Maravarman now win against that large army? He did not want to lose many men; so a direct frontal attack was ruled out. He, along with Selvam and Singaram, devised a "string of pearls" strategy. They decided to torment the enemy on multiple fronts.

One part of his army went to the Kaveri river, looking to cross it and make a lateral entry into the Chola kingdom. They made a lot of noise as they moved. They sure wanted the whole world to know they were on the move.

The section of the Chola army that went to the Kaveri had clear instructions to stop the Pandya army at the river. So there they were: two large armies camped opposite each other, a raging Kaveri separating them. The two opposing captains, Selvam from the Pandyas and Maruthu from the Cholas, stood looking at each other. The staring continued until Selvam started smiling. The smile gave way to a hearty laugh. Not an arrogant laugh, but a confident one. It appeared that he knew something the other party did not.

Neither army could move until the raging river subsided. So a waiting game began.

Selvam sent ten soldiers across the river. They swam through the gushing river and attacked the enemy sentries. Having made the point, they jumped back into the water, and were pulled back using ropes. Each day, the attack on the Cholas came from different points along the river. These attacks came during dawn, dusk and whenever else the sun got clouded out.

Admittedly, such attacks had only a small impact, but they were enough to irritate and provoke the Cholas.

Maruthu was planning his own attack. His men got ready to cross over at dawn the next day. Not five or ten men, but his entire platoon. Preparations were made in stealth. At the crack of dawn, his platoon managed to cross the river using boats and ropes. They reassembled on the opposite bank and rushed into the Pandya camp.

To find it empty!

The Pandya camp was empty. There was no one in the tents. Perplexed, the soldiers looked around. These Pandyas somehow got wind of our plans, and have either fled or moved back to attack us, they thought.

They stood there for a few minutes. Then they heard a slight rumble. Was it the sound of hooves? Were the Pandyas moving in for the attack? The Chola soldiers looked at each other and then at Maruthu. Maruthu was at a loss, too.

The sound kept getting louder, and the Chola platoon started moving back towards the bank and their boats. As they reached the bank, they identified the source of the sound. It was a flood. The river was in spate, and was rushing towards them. Not a single person had time to react. The entire platoon was washed away.

A few days ago, in total secrecy, one group of Pandya soldiers had moved upstream. Their only job was to identify the right spot to construct a temporary dam. The quickly-constructed dam ensured that a lot of water was stored over the next few days. At the right time, when Selvam gave them the signal, the men broke the dam. The water gushed out as per plan and wiped out the entire Chola platoon. Not a single loss in the Pandya camp.

A brilliant strategy, using the terrain and provoking the enemy into action. Luring them into a position of disadvanage.

Rajarajan had settled in well as the king. He had set everything right in his region. There was peace, in general, and things were moving on auto-pilot. This kind of smooth flow does allow a bit of complacence to creep in. Rajarajan had even acquired a slight paunch. Not just that. He had allowed a coterie of yes-men to form around him. Maruthu was a member of that coterie. Instead of leading from the front, Rajarajan had sent Maruthu to lead his army and was sending him instructions from the palace. Was that enough? Maruthu did have some war experience, but was he capable of leading a large army to victory over a mighty enemy? No.

This was why Selvam had laughed the other day, when he saw his opposite number standing across the Kaveri. He had marked out every commander the Cholas had. He knew their experience, strengths and limitations. Maruthu, he knew, lacked the battle experience and the cunning necessary to lead and win. He was predictable, and that was his deficiency.

Meanwhile, another part of Maravarman's army went to the big fort at Uraiyur. The same fort his father had lost to Rajarajan.

They encircled the fort and did the usual, cutting off communication and supplies. On their way to Uraiyur, they captured all the high points, supply routes and communication depots. Their arrival at the fort was expected, and yet, a surprise in terms of the speed.

But Rajarajan was not worried. He had ensured enough supplies for his subjects. He had factored in all possible scenarios.

The Pandyan archers started showering the fort with arrows. Rajarajan's men moved to the fort wall in defense. Inside the fort though, a small Pandya gang, moving in silence, started killing the Chola soldiers one by one. The soldiers were knifed and slowly lowered to the floor. All this, while the attention of the Chola soldiers was riveted on the ruckus outside the fort, where some Pandya soldiers were raining arrows while others were getting ready to break the large door of the fort.

The silent assassins inside the fort kept at their work. At long last, a sentry atop the fort noticed what was going on and raised the alarm. Suddenly, the Chola soldiers realised that they were being attacked from within! They jumped down and started fighting. But by this time, the entrance to the fort had been broken down and the Pandya forces had rushed in. Selvam's forces joined them. Together, they routed the Cholas.

Rajarajan had planned for all scenarios except for an attack from within. He did not know that some of the men inside the Uraiyur fort were actually loyal to the Hoysala kingdom. These were men who, after the previous war, had married Chola women and had stayed on in Uraiyur. Their allegiance, though, was clear: to the Hoysala king. While they lived as Chola subjects in peacetime, they proved to be "sleeper cells" that could be activated by the Hoysalas when the time came— as proved by their internal attack now.

Maravarman simply sent word to these sleeper cells to attack the Cholas at a specific time.

When Maravarman entered the fort after his forces had captured it, a shamefaced Rajarajan faced him as a prisoner. Maravarman wanted a complete victory. In the ensuing sword fight, he had no trouble eliminating Rajarajan.

Maravarman Sundara Pandyan avenged his father and reclaimed the Pandya kingdom.

The final chapter had been written in the war between the Cholas and the Pandyas.

Or had it?

* * *

The silhouette of a woman and a boy atop a hill.

The woman held the boy's hand as they looked yonder at the fort they had escaped from.

Dusk was setting in, and there were dark clouds above. It was going to rain.

However much it rains, it will not be enough to douse the fire burning within.

The woman reached behind her, picked up a sword and handed it to the boy.

Suganthi, the widow of Rajarajan III, held her son Rajendran II and said,

"Son, it is time for you to get ready. You must avenge the death of your father."

* * *

> **INTERPRETATION**
>
> - Plan for all scenarios, from outside and from within.

MOOVENDHAR: Helicopter Leadership, Anyone?

Anu: Leadership. That's what this story is about.

Gokul: And scenario-planning.

Rita: Yes. We must avoid favouritism. I am guilty of that, as are both of you. We have our golden-eyed proteges. The ones who can do no wrong! With that kind of halo, we think they will be superstars in any field or task.

Anu: We need to pick the right person for the right job, match their skills and capabilities with their aspiration. And their discipline.

Gokul: Yes. And we need to know who in our respective companies is idling: not working and not allowing others to work, either. In other words, being a saboteur within the fort walls.

JK: There's one more essential lesson from this story: razor-sharp focus and specific intention are the hallmarks of a leader.

You, as a leader, ought to avoid micro-management and the "remote-controlled helicopter" approach. Don't be a helicopter leader. Pick the right head for the right task. Let them develop an action plan, study the competition and take the right steps.

Keep running. Keep up the alternative learning. Knowledge comes from all sources. It is up to us to take it all in.

Observe. Analyse. Act.

The best win is where we win without fighting!

Marketing case in point

In the USA, the large airline companies had built strong hub-and-spoke models, with hubs in key metro cities. These hubs were developed like fortresses, making it difficult for any new competitor to enter. It would be expensive. And a new competitor would need a lot of time and effort to penetrate a big airline's base or replicate it.

So, instead of fighting the big airlines directly, Southwest Airlines selected small airports that were located *near* the main cities. In most cases, they selected small cities that were not covered by the big airlines. For instance, Chicago's O'Hare airport was United Airlines' hub, with over 1000 flights per day. So Southwest used the smaller Chicago Midway airport, instead. The brand established itself in the smaller cities of the USA.

Southwest created its own battle grounds and built a competitive advantage that was difficult for the established players to comprehend, let alone copy.

If you would like to have an audio version of the stories, mail outlier@pravinshekar.com for a copy.

SECTION 3

A PEEK INTO THE FUTURE: PANDYAS VS SOUTH INDIA!

An exclusive preview of the next book in this series.

Fight the Fight within, First

King Sundara Pandyan II was a frustrated man. Nothing seemed to work. Every initiative of his was a failure. Most of his men were not working to their full potential. His ministers seemed to be in a world of their own.

Was he staring at defeat again?

Sundaran was a young prince thrust into the limelight. The untimely demise of his father, King Sundara Pandyan I, had put him on the throne after a lot of struggle. At 24, he was young, but old enough to know what needed to be done. Already married, and with a kid on the way, he faced extra pressure to get things right.

His father, in the latter years of his life, had been a much-troubled man. There was war brewing everywhere. Sundara I had suffered a significant loss of territory and face. He died on the battlefield, trying to defend against an attack from the North.

Sundara II was young and restless, and wanted to bring back the peace and glory of his forefathers. He had been trained in equal measure to fight wars and rule justly. He felt quite lonely, though. He spent the mandatory mourning period thinking. He documented everything that his father had tried in the last few years. He made a list of his allies, current and potential. And the list of defectors and enemies. He arrived at a roadmap for the future.

He called his council of ministers and told them what had to be done. They received his plan with appreciation. Each minister picked up an initiative they would lead. It was a day of joy for Sundara, to have his plans accepted.

Every week, he asked for a status update. Apart from some little progress here and there, most of the initiatives stalled. Some were in freefall, with the actions implemented proving counter-productive. Sundara continued to lose territory. He pleaded, implored and threatened his ministers, but to no avail.

He brought in new ministers and advisers, hoping that they would bring about positive change. But most of them turned out to be non-performers, too. Some of them even left the kingdom on some pretext or the other.

>
> - New ideas and initiatives — stalled or dropped altogether.
> - Armament procurement and production — delayed.
> - New men for the army — not recruited.
> - Existing alliances — frayed.
> - New partnerships with neighboring kingdoms — rebuffed.
> - Defectors — more brazen and more in number.
> - Tax collection — low.
> - The morale of the population — lower!

Things came to such a stage that some people openly started questioning his capability as a king, as their saviour and leader. He began to doubt himself.

"Were my plans bad? Was my allocation and selection process imperfect? Should I go back to micro-managing?"

King Sundara Pandyan II was a frustrated man. Nothing seemed to work. Every initiative of his was a failure. Most of his men were not working to their full potential. His ministers seemed to be in a world of their own.

Was he staring at defeat again?

He went to a couple of elderly ex-ministers, who had retired from his father's war cabinet. They were living in the forest, as was customary in that era. After finishing their duty to king and country, they retired to the forest to live a life of penance and peace.

Vageesh and Baskar were the two ex-ministers Sundara consulted. They were happy to see him, and invited him to spend some time at their hermitage. Ah, days of peace and clarity! The ex-ministers understood the issues Sundara was facing, and discussed them threadbare.

Who sided with whom? What coteries possibly existed? What could the personal motivations of each person be? What political ploy could be enacted? How did Sundara take decisions? How were people involved in ideation and decision-making? What was the competition like? On and on they went like this for a few days.

This is what Sundara missed in his cabinet: his ministers and advisers questioning the plans, openly debating them, proposing their own ideas and helping him come up with the right solutions.

Sundaran left the hermitage with a clear idea of what could be, if he did whatever needed to be done.

He left with one key lesson on war and leadership.

Back in the palace, he recruited a small crack team, one that reported only to him in total secrecy. If it sounds Machiavellian, it was. Call them his secret informants. Sundara disguised himself and walked through his kingdom. He gained invaluable, first-hand knowledge about the plight of his people, and their wishes and aspirations. He also identified capable people (men and women) who could be groomed as leaders, ministers, commanders. He set up a shadow council of ministers, and together, they started solving problems one by one.

Approaches for alliance were made in secret, directly from him to other kings. He received letters of thanks, and understood how their words and messages had been misrepresented by his earlier council of ministers. Partnership pacts were sealed. Sundara spoke to a few defectors to find out the real reason for their defecting. They said it was the rot that had started setting in in his kingdom. They had left in frustration. He welcomed some of them back to take charge of specific areas that needed cleaning up.

His crack team continued to pick smart individuals, who were then trained and deployed.

Little by little, he reclaimed his kingdom — from himself, I dare say. A few ministers who showed promise were sent to Vageesh and Baskar for training. Change were implemented, one person and one small region at a time. Sundara focussed on rebuilding his tribe in a planned manner. Every area that saw a positive change spoke about it. Positive news takes time to spread, but is very rooted.

Did everything work? Of course not. There were some setbacks. Some lazy ministers, who just wanted power and authority, tried to scuttle these initiatives. Sundara's team of informants kept him appraised of such people, and they were eased out.

A total revamp of his cabinet and commanders. Sundara was on his way to a resurrection.

The big lesson he learnt at the hermitage was:

Quell the fight within, first.

A healthy body is needed for a healthy mind, and vice versa. For a kingdom, a strong population and self-belief are vital. Viruses need to be removed, the body exercised, and defectors and trouble-makers eliminated. Only then can a king rule well.

Fight the fight within, first.

* * *

Now relate Sundara's situation with your business or career. All your good intentions and plans seem to be floundering. None of the plans seem to be executed. The people around you seem to lack your drive. Things seem to be going against your goals. Frustration and teeth-gnashing have set in, but they don't help.

What can you do to get things back on track?

Set up a crack team focused on clear objectives, align them to your goals, give them micro-steps to complete.

One small step at a time, in the right direction.

The (Marketing) Warrior without Vanity

Like a storm that comes without notice,
he rages through his enemies.
Before they know what hit them,
they would have met their maker.

A warrior who knows that the real power of victory
lies in stealth and surprise.
And so he remains masked,
as do his warriors.

The masked bandits who strike at will,
killing only those armed.
Taking nothing other than the victory
and allegiance of the people to their new king.

When he comes,
and how
is never known.
That's the way he wants it.

For the real power lies in the mystery,
the aura and the myth.
The reality, though,
is quite different.

He refuses to be named
or recognised.
The only incentive being
the freedom to do as he wills.

Just, ethical and extremely economical
in word, deed and expense.
Striking only when he knows victory is certain.
Often, his mere presence guarantees a victory

without bloodshed.
Can victory be any sweeter?

About the Author – Pravin Shekar

Pravin Shekar is an Outlier Marketer and a raconteur.

Unconventional marketing is his forte. When the world moves one way, you need to move another way: that's his philosophy. This going-against-the-grain attitude helps him find opportunity in every crisis.

A recipient of the American Marketing Association's "Emerging Leader" award, Pravin is passionate about marketing and believes that micro-marketing can redefine the business environment.

When you need to shake up your marketing strategy and re-gear your growth, reach out to him at mic@pravinshekar.com & www.linkedin.com/in/pravinshekar

Pravin Shekar's books:
https://pravinshekar.com/books/

MARKETING

- DEVIL DOES CARE: Outlier Marketing for Bootstrapped Entrepreneurs

- HOW TO GET MY FIRST PAID SPEAKING GIG!

- VIRTUAL SUMMIT PLAYBOOK: A Guide to Hosting Your Own Online Conference.

- CLIMB YOUR WAY OUT OF HELL: Outlier Marketing to Overcome Worst-case Scenarios and Grow Your Business

- THE GHATOTKACHA GAME: Marketing Lessons from Mythology

TALK-BOOK

- OPHTHALMOLOGISTS BRAND YOURSELF!

CREATIVITY

- WITH YOU, FOR YOU: A Collection of Travel Images and Romantic Poems

- LOVE IS JUST A PAGE AWAY: Short Stories from the Heart

Thanks

My sincere thanks to:

- My tribe of outlier marketers
- My designer-in-crime team from Mojocanvas: Arun and Nandhini Ramkumar
- Editor Ganesh Vancheeswaran
- My idea bounce/review team of TNC Venkatarangan, Marketer Rajesh Srinivasan, Gokul Santhanam, Ravi Venkatramani
- The Nanowrimo team from the Professional Speakers Association of India
- My publisher NotionPress, Project Manager Swetha and the team
- My team at Krea eKnowledge and Krux108
- Amma, Anu and my family

OTHER BOOKS BY PRAVIN SHEKAR

Pick up a copy of:

THE GHATOTKACHA GAME

MARKETING LESSONS FROM MYTHOLOGY

Are there any lessons?

Would it be a stretch to connect the dots, to learn marketing from stories of yore, from characters that have been chiselled and enhanced across centuries?

A marketer seeks inspiration from all possible sources, including ones that are clearly outliers! Let us take one particular character from the Mahabharata.

Ghatotkacha is a very powerful character in Indian mythology. Everything from Ghatotkacha's birth to his death is a game. Does he play different games, or is he a part of one himself?

As a marketer, what can I learn from his life? What can I implement and what can I share?

After reading this book, ask yourself: did Ghatotkacha play games, or did he participate in the success of a bigger game?

The parallels drawn in the book are the authors' own, based on two decades of marketing various services, products and solutions.

The authors believe and evangelise that each of us, first and foremost, is a marketer. This facet has to be brought to the front, and in unusual ways. This book is one such effort.

Marketing. Mythology. And the many messages therein.

Pick up your copy today.

QR CODE and site link

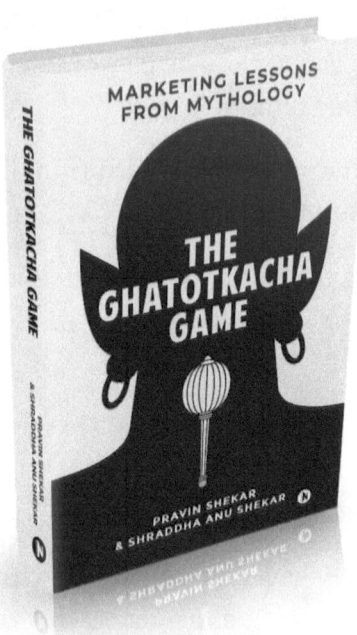

Other Books by Pravin Shekar

Other Books by Pravin Shekar

Other Books by Pravin Shekar

Other Books by Pravin Shekar

Other Books by Pravin Shekar

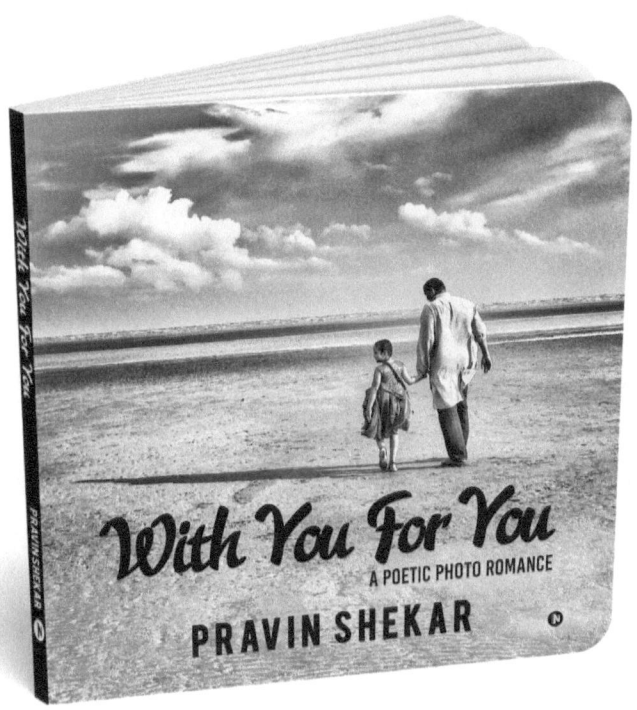

www.ingramcontent.com/pod-product-compliance
Lightning Source LLC
Chambersburg PA
CBHW020912180526
45163CB00007B/2707